EXOTIC FOOD THE CRAFTY WAY

MICHAEL BARRY

THE ERSKINE PRESS

for JARROLD PUBLISHING

NORWICH

EXOTIC FOOD THE CRAFTY WAY

Designed and produced by
THE ERSKINE PRESS
Banham, Norwich
for JARROLD PUBLISHING
Norwich

Recipes by Michael Barry
Food for photography by
The Banham Bakehouse, Norfolk
Food styling by Lesley de Boos
Photography © by Andrew Perkins
Designed by Stephen Easton
Flowers by Jonny

Text copyright © Michael Barry 1996
This edition copyright © Jarrold Publishing 1996
ISBN 0–7117–0855–X

Printed in England

CONTENTS

INTRODUCTION

Exoticness comes easily to me; I was born exotic you see, being half Welsh and half Indian. From my earliest memories of family meals rice has always played as large a part as potatoes. My father could, and sometimes did, eat a pound of rice at a sitting and had the true rice lover's belief that *real* food could only be served with rice. My mother, who is a skilled and instinctive cook, not only learned the kormas and raitas of my father's native cuisine, but used it as jumping off ground for round the world explorations. We travelled to many countries in reality and to even more in the kitchen. This was wonderful for me: not only was I an enthusiastic (greedy) little boy, but as I grew up exotic food seemed normal. New tastes and textures, unusual combinations were an expected part of life rather than a novel experience.

Broadcasting, my main work, has taken me all over the world and I have had the chance to live and work in the West Indies and in Africa. And so, to a childhood training and initiation were added the most wonderful opportunities to see and shop in eastern and tropical markets, to go out with fishermen into the Indian Ocean and the Caribbean Sea, to have avocados and limes and mangoes growing in my garden.

Living in exotic climes is very different from being a tourist and tourists usually only come across those foods which are most amenable to their palates; it may be exotic but it probably won't be extreme. And it is exactly this kind of acceptable and instantly likeable exotic food that this book contains. Easy, tasty, quick and with enough of a difference and tang to make each mouthful a bit of an adventure.

This is not a scholar's book, full of minute detail and footnotes but it is a cook's book, looking for cookability and flavour. It's also a crafty cook's book – where it is possible to simplify, I have. Where a food processor can replace a pestle and mortar, it does. Where a difficult ingredient doesn't make much difference, it is left out but only and *only* if the result is good to eat and in its essence captures the flavour and the textures of the original.

I hope everything in the book is easy to cook and I especially hope you will find the dishes truly to your taste. They are my pick of a lifetime's love of exotic eating. Don't treat the recipes with too much trepidation. If you can't find an ingredient, substitute. If you want to combine dishes from different parts of the world, do – food is fun, and freedom to experiment is part of the pleasure. I have also suggested outlines of how meals are put together in different parts of the world, so if you want a South East Asian or South American pattern to your saté or baby beef you can have one. If you have half as much pleasure in discovering, cooking and sampling these recipes as I have had over the years, I envy you the voyage of discovery you are about to start. *Bon voyage!*

INGREDIENTS

Amchoor: This is a powder made from dried mangoes. It's used as a flavouring with dhals and pulses all over the Indian sub-continent and has a slightly fruity, sour note which brings out their flavour. It's available in good Indian or Asian grocers.

Attar Flour: A fine-ground wholemeal flour used for making Indian breads, available from Indian grocers; crucial for great parathas.

Chillies: A wide variety of chilli is grown worldwide. They range from mild or sweet to stunningly hot. In Britain, the most widely available are the larger sized red and green chillis and the lantern-shaped 'Scotch bonnet' chillis which are both medium to hot. Tinned and dried chillis are also available. Look for the Mexican Jalapeno variety which have flavour as well as heat. Dried, powdered chillis are sold as chilli powder and chilli pepper; these are usually straight powdered dried chilli but can be spice mixtures as well. Chilli sauces range from the sweet and garlicky South East Asian variety – look for Linghams – to West African tongue splitters – Encona – to West Indian dissolved essence of chilli like Pickapeppa or Tabasco. Always use chilli to your taste. Red and green chillis are now available pre-ground and fresh in jars.

Chinese Cabbage: There are five or six different kinds of Chinese cabbage eaten widely in China, ranging from something that resembles a very delicate form of broccoli up to the thick celery-type Chinese leaves that we are used to in Britain. Spring greens are closer to the rather leafy and delicate kind of Chinese cabbage that's needed for some dishes. A variety of these sorts of greens can be found in good Chinese supermarkets in the Chinatowns of our larger cities.

Coconut Milk: This is the creamy liquid that results from adding boiling water to grated coconut. However, it is possible to buy coconut milk in tins, which is very thick and flavourful; and in block form, rather like white margarine. This is not so good in flavour but widely available and easy to store. It needs mixing with hot water to create coconut cream.

Curry powder and curry spices: Curry powder is essentially a western convenience food. Most people in India and Asia make their own mixtures to match the dish. To make a basic Indian curry powder which can be kept in an air-tight tin, mix ground quantities of:

4 tsp coriander seed (orangey and mild); 4 tsp cumin seed (pungent and fragrant); 3 tsp turmeric (very mild – mainly used for colour); 2 tsp ginger (hot and aromatic); 1 tbs chilli powder (very hot and pungent); 2 tsp cardamom seed (fragrant and delicate but lasting); 2 tsp black pepper (an original Indian spice); 2 tsp garam masala (a ready mixed group of sweet spices); 2 tsp cinnamon (sweet and fragrant). Use a tablespoon to 450 g (1 lb) of meat, chicken, fish or vegetable.
Curry pastes are now widely available in many varieties. I usually use about half the recommended quantities.

Dashi: This is the basic Japanese stock used for soups and other forms of cooking. It's quite complicated to make so it is really more practical to buy ready-made Dashi in a dried or powdered form, available in all Japanese supermarkets and many health food stores.

Dhals: Dhals are lentils and come in a variety of sizes and colours. They are all to be found in health food shops and oriental grocers.
Chana dhal 1: chick peas – 6 hours soaking, 1½ hours cooking.
Chana dhal 2: split yellow peas – no soaking, 40 minutes cooking.
Toor dhal: oiled split peas – 45 minutes cooking.
Urid dhal: black coated, white centre, sold whole or split – no soaking, 25–30 minutes cooking.
Masoor dhal: little red lentils – 25–30 minutes cooking.

Dried Mushrooms: These come in various sizes and are expensive. They need 20 minutes soaking in warm water.
Woodears, Cloudears – thin, flat mushrooms used mainly for texture
Shitake – Japanese button mushrooms, good flavour
Dried cepes – rich flavoured, expensive, button shaped mushrooms, usually in slices.

Dried Shrimps: Small, shelled, shrivelled shrimps sold by weight and found in Chinese food shops. Very pungent and used in small quantities as a flavouring.

Fish Sauce: This is used rather as we would use salt as a seasoning rather than as a central flavouring ingredient, although it varies from country to country in its pungency and fishiness. It's available in almost all Chinese or Asian supermarkets and looks very like soy sauce; it comes from Thailand or Vietnam.

Five Spice Powder: This is a basic Chinese spice mixture which can vary slightly but essentially has in it five sweet spices based on aniseed.

Fresh Prepared Spices: It's now possible to buy a range of exotic spices in their fresh form ready prepared for use. This is very similar to the kind of service you might get in a Singapore market where garlic, ginger and chillis can all be crushed or chopped to requirements when you buy them. All supermarkets now stock a range of garlic, ginger, chillis, lemon grass, and often other exotic flavours, that you can spoon straight from a jar kept in the fridge. It makes for wonderful easy cooking – don't be ashamed of it.

Ghee: Clarified butter in the Indian style. Put 225 g (8 oz) butter to melt in a saucepan. When melted, simmer for 15 minutes then pour the clear oil into a clean bowl and discard the white residue.

Ginger: Fresh root ginger is widely available. It needs to be peeled before use and keeps well in the fridge. Ginger also comes candied, in syrup and in dried and powdered form and fresh, crushed in jars.

Green Coriander: A leafy green herb that looks like parsley but has a more dramatic and lemony flavour. You can grow it or buy it from good greengrocers.

Hoisin Sauce: This is a thick soy based sauce always bought and used ready-made, even in China, which has an added sweetness to it and a strong garlic and savoury flavour. Sometimes it has sesame seeds added as well. It's used as a barbecue coating and as an ingredient in many Chinese dishes, and as a dip with Peking Duck.

Ikan: Dried, tiny fish, found in Chinese and oriental shops. It is used as a relish.

Kombu: Japanese edible seaweed used for making dashi – the basic Japanese stock.

Laos Powder: Also known as galangal and the 'lesser ginger', this has a slightly lemony taste and can be bought in fresh, dried and powdered forms from most good spice merchants.

Lemon Grass: Resembling dried spring onions, lemon grass releases a pungent citrus flavour into soups or sauces in a wide variety of South East Asian cooking. Can be found in many supermarkets and speciality shops selling vegetables. Also available ready crushed and fresh in jars.

Oyster Sauce: This is a form of soy sauce which has been made with oysters so that it has a mildly fishy taste. It has the texture and appearance of a slightly thickened soy sauce and can be eaten as it comes, poured over a variety of mild or steamed dishes.

Palm Oil: (Dende) A thick orange-yellow oil used in West African cooking as much for flavour as for frying. To be found in West African market stalls or shops.

Sake and Mirin: Dry and sweet versions of Japanese rice wine. Dry sherry and apple juice are the most used substitutes.

Sesame Oil: The oil from preserved sesame seeds. Widely used raw as a frying oil and as a flavouring when roasted for Chinese and Japanese soups and vegetable dishes.

Shrimp Paste: This is made by salting and drying tiny shrimps and then grinding them into a paste. It's used as a flavour intensifier rather than as a flavour in its own right and it is worked into sauces as varied as Saté Peanut Sauce and some salad dressings.

Soy Sauces:
Chinese soy sauce is made from fermented soya beans and comes in:
Light – uncooked; Heavy – boiled and reduced.
Hoisin sauce, a paste-like soy sauce with garlic and spices, is used to thicken sauces and act as a dip for Peking Duck and other poultry.
Japanese soy sauce – Shoyu – is made from soya beans and wheat. Beware some health shop versions which may not have been made in Japan; the best of all commercial soys is Japanese Kikoma.
Miso is a paste made from soya beans and other grains, and used to flavour soups.

Star Anise: This is used widely in Chinese cooking and is one of the main ingredients in five spice powder. It is so called because the seeds of the plant group themselves into attractive star clusters. You can use them whole or just use the shiny mahogany-coloured seeds from inside.

Sumac: This is a dark red powder used in Turkey, Iran and parts of Northern India as a condiment, rather as we would use pepper, sprinkled over food when it has been cooked.

Tamarind Water: The tamarind pulp is mixed with water and then strained to produce a sour juice slightly less puckering than plain lemon juice. You can buy dried tamarind in blocks in Indian and Chinese grocery shops and some health food stores. Also fresh tamarind is available in jars.

Tofu: Another soya product, this time white in colour and bland in flavour. It is high in protein and low in fat. Available in Chinese supermarkets and health food stores, it can be sold fresh, in packs or loose; dried or deep fried. It is used to replace meat or fish.

REGIONAL MEALS

African Meals: These vary from area to area. In some areas of eastern and western central Africa, the meal can be shared from a central pot. Soups are served as a main as well as a starter course.

Chinese Meals: These are normally served as one course consisting of rice with a soup, a vegetable dish, some meat or poultry and some fish. The dishes are chosen for a contrast of crisp and soft, spicy and mild, wet and dry.

Indian Meals: These are traditionally eaten with the fingers of the (carefully washed) right hand. The food is picked up with a small ball of rice or piece of bread and conveyed to the mouth. Dishes are put on the table in twos and threes and usually consist of one meat dish, one vegetable, a pulse or dhal dish and rice and/or chapattis. Accompaniments are chutneys and salads.

Japanese Meals: These can be taken as a series of courses – each with a number of very small-scale dishes served at the same time. Raw fish will open proceedings and rice, pickles and tea will always finish anything more substantial than a snack or fast food meal. Detail in table setting and food arrangement are central to Japanese meals.

Mexican and South American Meals: South American meals tend to follow the European pattern, with starters followed by main courses and sweets. However, some national dishes like the Brazilian Fejada require six or seven composite dishes to be served at the same time.

South East Asian Meals: Though Thai and Malaysian/Indonesian foods differ a little in their tastes and styles, all use a single course for a meal. This is based on a central serving of rice, with soup or very wet vegetable, a meat or fish curry, a dish with noodles and a variety of relishes, pickled salads, salted fish and nuts.

West Indian Meals: Family meals follow British patterns of soup and main course with vegetable and rice or potatoes. Grand meals tend to be more buffet-style with a number of dishes plus relishes and salads being served at once.

Thai hot prawn soup

Soups

To declare an interest from the start, I'm a soup man myself. I find the variety of textures, ingredients, flavours and, dare I say it, liquidity, of the world's soups a never-ending source of pleasure and discovery. I've given a small selection of my great favourites here: I hope you'll find that they all have a sufficiently distinctive taste and texture to contribute a unique course to your meals. One or two of them, like the Singapore Lakhsa or the Nigerian River Province Chicken Pot, are in fact meals in themselves. Some, like the golden, South American Pumpkin Soup or the Hot and Sour Soup from Hunaan Province in China, are meant as a prelude to other dishes. Some are meant to stimulate the appetite, like the Hot Thai Prawn and Chilli, some are meant to satisfy it, like the Japanese Noodle Bowl. What they all have in common is that they are easy to make and very economical.

Soup is something that can be said to separate cultures and communities. For some, soup is a basic food, something which appears at every meal and is essential to life. Other cultures do not feature soups in their cuisine at all; the idea of drinking hot liquid from a bowl with a spoon is totally alien. It could be that in most of those cultures where soup is unknown, spoons and eating utensils are traditionally also pretty rare. India, with its ancient custom of eating each meal off a fresh banana leaf in order to avoid contamination, and eating with the hand using no tools at all, would be unlikely to have soup as a central part of its cuisine. And the truth is that the only soups on the Indian sub-continent have been introduced by recent European rulers. In China and Japan, on the other hand, where meals have been eaten out of porcelain bowls for centuries, soup plays a central part of each 'proper' meal.

Do try to serve these soups in bowls that are appropriate. Chinese bowls seem to enhance Chinese or other oriental soups, whereas solid earthenware is suitable for the most robust offerings of the Caribbean or Africa.

THAI HOT PRAWN SOUP
(Tom Yam Kung)

This is perhaps the most famous dish in the whole of Thai cuisine and certainly the one that visitors are most likely to have been offered. In Thailand it's cooked in a steamboat, which is a little charcoal burner that is placed on a table with a moat around it in which the soup is both cooked and served. If you can find such a wonderful device in a local Chinese or eastern shop then by all means use it, but the soup tastes just as delicious served from a large tureen which could be kept warm over a little candle burner. Traditionally this soup is made just with prawns but you can, if you like, add other shellfish or firm-fleshed white fish to enrich and vary the recipe. It's meant to be served so that each diner gets more than one bowlful, so be sure to make enough.

2 stalks lemon grass
10 ml (1 dsp) Laos powder
(see Ingredients, page 6)
3 fresh red chillies (approx. 2.5–5 cm/1–2 in long), trimmed
1.4 litres (2½ pints) water
30 ml (2 tbs) fish sauce (see Ingredients, page 5) or use 5 ml (1 tsp) Worcester Sauce

700 g (1½ lb) raw prawns (heads removed)
15 ml (1 tbs) lemon or lime juice
3 citrus leaves (optional)
100 g (4 oz) button mushrooms, washed, trimmed and sliced
2 cloves garlic, peeled and chopped
30 ml (2 tbs) chopped coriander

Crush the lemon grass and add it, with the Laos powder and the chillies, to the water. Bring to the boil and simmer for 15 minutes. Add the fish sauce and the prawns (or the fish and prawns) and simmer for another 5 minutes until the prawns are pink and the fish is cooked. Add the lemon or lime juice, the citrus leaves, torn into postage stamp-sized pieces, and the button mushrooms. Leave off the heat for 1 minute while you quickly fry the chopped garlic in a smear of oil. Pour the soup into a warmed tureen. Add the fried garlic and the chopped coriander and serve.

Jamaican fish tea

JAMAICAN FISH TEA

Despite its name, this is really quite a thick soup. In Jamaica, any liquid that doesn't contain alcohol and is derived from 'brewing' a substance in water is called tea. This solid and nutritious soup is made in the fishing villages along the Jamaican coast. One of the key ingredients is green bananas which are ordinary bananas eaten before they ripen, when they have a texture much more like that of potato than of the sweet fruit we are familiar with. They are easily obtained in any market that caters for ethnic tastes as they are a common ingredient in African as well as West Indian cooking. The fish can be the trimmings and offcuts that most fishmongers will sell you at a very reduced price as they are otherwise thrown away.

900 g (2 lb) fish pieces, including heads and bones
1 chilli pepper (the round West Indian kind known as Scotch Bonnet is traditional)
1 sprig thyme
1.7 litres (3 pints) water

700 g (1½ lb) green bananas, peeled and cut into 1 cm (½ in) chunks
1 large tomato, skinned and chopped
1 bunch spring onions, trimmed and cut into 5 mm (¼ in) lengths
seasoning

Wash the fish pieces and put them with the whole uncut chilli and the thyme into the water. Bring to the boil, cover and turn down to a very low simmer for 45 minutes. Strain the liquid through a fine sieve and to it add the green bananas, the chopped tomato and the spring onions. Bring back to the boil and simmer for 15–20 minutes until the bananas are tender. You can add any flakes of fish from the debris in the sieve to the soup as well. Season to taste and serve hot.

BRAZILIAN PUMPKIN SOUP

Pumpkins are a favourite soup vegetable all over the world but there is no question that the best pumpkin soups and the biggest variety of pumpkins come from Central and South America, where pumpkins were first grown. This soup is a speciality of the Bahia cuisine in Brazil, but similar soups, with local variations, are made all over South America. The colour, the flavour and the texture provided by the pumpkin is just irresistible.

225 g (8 oz) onion, peeled and chopped
2 cloves garlic, peeled and chopped
100 g (4 oz) tomatoes, peeled and chopped
50 g (2 oz) butter
1 pinch each salt and sugar

1 litre (2 pints) stock (beef is traditional but chicken stock or even water can be used)
700 g (1½ lb) pumpkin, peeled and cut into small dice
2.5 ml (½ tsp) Tabasco sauce

Cook the chopped onion, garlic and tomatoes in the butter for 5 minutes. Season with salt and sugar, then add the stock or water. Add the pumpkin, bring to the boil and simmer for 20 minutes. The pumpkin will have partially disintegrated and the soup is traditionally eaten without any further sieving but you can, if you prefer, process it briefly to mix the vegetables together. Don't make it absolutely smooth as the texture is quite important. Add the Tabasco and serve.

CANTONESE CHICKEN AND SWEETCORN SOUP

This is the classic soup of Chinese restaurants in this country but it is none the worse for that. It's a very simple soup to make and is generally acceptable to children not used to exotic foods, as well as to those with more sophisticated palates. It can also be made with white crab meat instead of chicken, in approximately the same proportions. The crab meat needs to be added only three minutes before serving, as it has already been cooked.

1 medium onion, peeled and finely chopped
2.5 cm (1 in) piece fresh root ginger, peeled and finely chopped
30 ml (2 tbs) cooking oil
1 pinch five spice powder (see Ingredients, page 6)
800 ml (1½ pints) chicken stock (good quality cube will do, but fresh is better)

350 g (12 oz) sweetcorn kernels (frozen or tinned)
25 g (1 oz) cornflour
1 chicken breast cut into very small dice (or 225 g (8 oz) white crab meat)
4 spring onions, trimmed and finely chopped

Fry the chopped onion and ginger gently in the oil for 3 minutes. Add the five spice powder, the stock and the sweetcorn and bring to the boil; cover and simmer for 15 minutes. Mix the cornflour with a little water and stir into the soup. Bring back to the boil and remove from the heat. Put 2 ladlefuls of the soup (225 ml/8 fl oz) into a food processor or liquidizer and process until smooth. Return to the soup with the diced chicken breast and simmer for a further 5 minutes. If using crab meat, add it 2–3 minutes before serving and stir into the soup thoroughly. Garnish with the finely chopped spring onions and serve in Chinese bowls.

HUNAAN HOT AND SOUR SOUP

Sweet and sour is not much of a tradition in real Chinese cooking but hot and sour is. The combinations of chilli- and vinegar-based flavours are regarded as having a very stimulating effect on the appetite. This is a marvellous soup for cold weather which, we often forget, China experiences plenty of, particularly in the more northern provinces like Hunaan. I use one of the exotic frozen vegetable mixes available from supermarkets to make this soup because the combination of peas, carrots, red pepper and celery is ideal. If you prefer to start with fresh vegetables and prepare your own dice, that's an excellent alternative and is, of course, the way they do actually make it in China.

1 large onion, peeled and finely chopped
225 g (8 oz) exotic mixed vegetables, diced (see above)
2.5 ml (½ tsp) five spice powder (see Ingredients, page 6)
2.5 ml (½ tsp) ground ginger
cooking oil

100 g (4 oz) cooked beef, cut into small cubes (optional)
1 litre (2 pints) beef stock (Oxo cubes won't do!)
15 ml (2 tbs) soy sauce
25 g (1 oz) cornflour
15 ml (2 tbs) cider vinegar
5 ml (1 tsp) Tabasco or chilli garlic sauce

Fry the onion, mixed vegetables, five spice powder and ginger in the oil gently for 4 minutes. Add the beef, if using, and the beef stock and cook for another 10 minutes. Mix the soy sauce, cornflour, vinegar and chilli sauces together until smooth. Add to the soup off the heat, stir thoroughly and bring back to a gentle boil for 5 minutes until the soup thickens. Test for seasoning and for the balance of sourness. The soup should be spicy and sharp but not mouth puckering. A little spring onion green, chopped coriander, or chopped parsley can be sprinkled on the top as a garnish.

NIGERIAN RIVER PROVINCE CHICKEN SOUP

Different versions of this soup are made all over West Africa and they vary in spiciness and content from region to region. The River Province of Nigeria is known for particularly vivid spicing so you may want to reduce the amount of chilli in your first attempt. Nigerian recipes are often quite short on specific instructions and have an unusual measurement unit which is the cigarette tin. This is a hangover from the time when cigarettes were sold in Nigeria in the kind of rounded or oval tins, containing 25 or 50 cigarettes, that used to be available in this country in my childhood. Therefore instructions like, 2 cigarette tins of prepared spinach, that are to be found in even modern Nigerian recipes, I take to mean about 450 g (1 lb) spinach. I have however – to your relief no doubt – translated the quantities in this particular version of the recipe. In Nigeria the soup is eaten very thick, often with a kind of bread made from Cassava, but for our consumption it should have the consistency of a good thick minestrone.

225 g (8 oz) raw chicken, plus the bones or carcass of the bird
100 ml (4 fl oz) oil (palm oil, the rich red West African cooking oil, is specified but ordinary cooking oil can be used)
225 g (8 oz) tomatoes, peeled and chopped

100 g (4 oz) onions, peeled and chopped
8 ml (1 heaped tsp) chilli powder
450 g (1 lb) washed spinach (frozen will do)
50 g (2 oz) cooked peeled prawns
salt and freshly ground pepper

Cut the chicken meat into fine dice, discarding any small bones. Put the bones or chicken carcass into a large saucepan, cover with 1.4–1.7 litres (2½–3 pints) of water. Bring to the boil and simmer for 40 minutes to reduce the stock. In a separate pan heat the oil or palm oil and add the tomatoes, onions, chilli powder and chicken meat; cook gently together for 15 minutes. Slice the washed spinach into thin ribbons and add to the stewing vegetables with the prawns. Turn and mix thoroughly and add the chicken stock, a ladleful at a time, until the soup reaches the desired consistency. Check it for seasoning before serving.

JAPANESE MISO SOUP

Miso is a form of very thick fermented bean paste. It is produced and eaten all over Japan but was very little known outside its country of origin until recently. It seems to be one of those foods which have all the ingredients necessary to make them the constituent of a healthy diet – low in fat, low in sugar, high in protein, good in fibre – and therefore it is now possible to buy miso in health food shops anywhere in Britain. It comes in a variety of flavours and intensities from quite mild to very dark and rich. I suggest you look for a fairly mild and light coloured miso for this particular soup. Soup is always part of a Japanese meal, and whether it is breakfast, lunch or dinner, especially in home cooking, that soup is always a miso soup. Traditionally the soup is made from a stock called dashi, made from the unusual ingredients of a kind of seaweed and dried flakes from the bonito fish. If you are lucky enough to be close to a Japanese shop they will be able to supply it in a ready-prepared dried form. If not, use a light chicken stock.

225 g (8 oz) fresh green stringless beans, trimmed and cut into 5 cm (2 in) lengths 800 ml (1½ pints) chicken stock or dashi stock (see Ingredients, page 5)

100 g (4 oz) button or shitake mushrooms, washed, trimmed and cut into 5 mm (¼ in) slices 15 ml (1 tbs) medium to light miso

Put the beans into the stock, bring to the boil and simmer for 4 minutes. Add the mushrooms and simmer for another 2 minutes. Put the miso into a cup and stir until smooth. Take a ladleful of stock from the soup and add to the miso, stirring until it is thoroughly blended (as you would cornflour). Tip the ingredients of the cup into the soup, stir thoroughly, bring just to the boil and switch off. Do not boil the soup after this point, but check it after adding the miso for saltiness. Some misos are much saltier than others and may need no further seasoning. Serve the soup hot into bowls.

KYOTO NOODLE BOWL

Noodles are to Japan what almost all other kinds of fast food are to the rest of the world. There are noodle bars where we would find a hamburger joint. There are noodle bars where we would expect to find a café or a fish and chip shop. The meals that are served in them are always served in individual portions but the portions are very large, as a bowl of soup noodles is an alternative to a full meal. The ingredients vary and can range from very simple, totally vegetarian dishes with just bean curd and one or two vegetable flavourings to complex concoctions which include fish and meat. This is a simple but, I think, delicious mixture which I first tasted at a noodle bar in the railway station of Japan's ancient capital Kyoto.

350 g (12 oz) Japanese noodles or thick spaghetti
50 g (2 oz) mushrooms, washed and trimmed
1 litre (2 pints) fresh chicken stock
30 ml (2 tbs) soy sauce
2 carrots, peeled and thinly sliced across the grain

large raw chicken breast, boned and skinned and thinly sliced across the grain
4 spring onions, topped and tailed and cut into 5 mm (¼ in) lengths
225 g (8 oz) fresh spinach, cut in 1 cm (½ in) ribbons
4 eggs

Put 1.7 litres (3 pints) of water in a large saucepan, bring it to the boil, then add a pinch of salt and the noodles. Boil for 3 minutes, cover and leave to stand for another 7 minutes and then drain. Criss-cross the tops of the mushrooms like a noughts-and-crosses board with a sharp knife. To cook: put a cup of the stock into a saucepan with half the soy sauce. Add the carrots, bring to the boil and simmer for 5 minutes. Add the chicken slices and the spring onions and simmer for a further 5 minutes. Place the spinach ribbons in the remaining chicken stock and bring to the boil. Add the rest of the soy sauce, the chicken and carrot mixture, and the mushrooms, and simmer for 2 minutes. Divide the noodles into 4 large individual soup bowls and ladle the vegetable and chicken mixture onto them, making sure that everybody gets an even share of the mushrooms, chicken and vegetables; top up afterwards with the soup, which should be at boiling point. Break an egg into each bowl, then cover with a plate and leave for 3 minutes for the egg to set before serving.

Kyoto noodle bowl

VENEZUELAN BLACK BEAN SOUP

Although the recipe for this Venezuelan dish specifies black beans, and they are surprisingly easily available in Britain in supermarkets and health food stores, you could get away with doing it with red beans which are a first cousin. The 'dende' or palm oil in the recipe is a special thick, dark red oil used in the area as much for flavour as it is for its culinary properties. It is to a certain extent an acquired taste. Ordinary salad oil produces the same texture without the flavour.

225 g (8 oz) black beans
1 beef stock cube
2 cloves of garlic
1 large onion

1 large fresh tomato (or 2 medium ones)
croutons
15 ml (1 tbsp) oil (preferably 'dende' or palm oil)
salt and pepper

Soak the beans for 6 hours then drain and rinse. Chop the onion and garlic finely and add to the beans. Dissolve the stock cube in enough water to cover the beans, onions and garlic by 3 inches (probably about a pint and a half). Bring to the boil and boil for 10 minutes. Simmer for 1½ hours on top of the stove or in a medium oven, 325°F/170°C/160C Fan/Gas 3/top of the Aga slow oven. Remove about half of the mixture and purée it in a blender or food processor, then replace into the soup. Rough chop the tomato and add to the soup with the oil. Season generously and mix in thoroughly, adding more water if it is too thick. Serve hot with croutons and parsley.

PEA SOUP FROM BARBADOS

Very different from the European style of pea soup, Caribbean peas are actually beans. They are known variously in the different islands as congo or gungo or pigeon peas but actually they look a bit like large haricot beans with black or dark red spots. You can buy them dried or tinned and the soup they make has a richness and creaminess that is set off beautifully by the still slightly crunchy vegetables cooked with it.

225 g (8 oz) dried or 450 g (1 lb) tinned cooked pigeon peas
100 g (4 oz) each peeled onion and carrot
100 g (4 oz) trimmed celery

750 ml (1½ pints) water or chicken stock
1 small chilli pepper
seasoning

If the peas are dried you soak them for 6 hours in plenty of water and then, in fresh water, bring to the boil for 10 minutes and cook them gently for an hour without salt until they are tender. You just have to open a tin if you're using the tinned version! Add the cooked peas to the water or chicken stock with the de-seeded chilli. Season generously and bring to the boil again. Put into a food processor or liquidizer and purée. Finely chop the onion, carrot and celery but leave it with some texture. Add to the puréed soup, cook for 5 minutes, check for seasoning and serve.

WEST INDIAN CALLALLOO AND CRAB SOUP

Callalloo is the name used in Trinidad and Tobago for spinach, although it's not the same variety as we recognise here. Both traditional spinach, New Zealand type spinach and chard or silver beet spinach are all satisfactory for this recipe, although callalloo itself has a slightly more creamy texture when cooked and puréed. In the same way, the crabs they use in the Caribbean are slightly different from the ones we have on British shores but the final product is equally delicious.

450 g (1 lb) spinach (or callaloo)
225 g (8 oz) fresh crab meat (white and
brown), cooked
225 g (8 oz) onions
750 ml (1½ pints) chicken stock

pinch of nutmeg
50 g (2 oz) butter
1 lime
seasoning

Wash the spinach and fry with the finely chopped onion in the butter. Season generously, add the stock and the nutmeg and simmer for 10 minutes. Liquidise the mixture until smooth, add the crab meat and squeeze in the lime juice. Serve immediately without reheating.

AVOCADO AND ZUCCHINI SOUP

The west coast of South America, with its two long thin countries of Peru and Chile, has some unusual cooking and very strong European influences. This is partly because it was this coast of America that the Spanish concentrated on for centuries after Columbus discovered the continent for them. The style of the people, the cities and the food therefore often has a quite European feel. Most of the ingredients for this delicious and light soup originate, however, not in Europe but north of Peru and Chile in the Mexican Yucatan area.

750 ml (1½ pints) chicken stock
225 g (8 oz) courgettes
2 large ripe avocados
100 ml (4 fl oz) plain yoghurt
45 ml (3 tbsp) freshly squeezed lemon juice
10 ml (2 tsp) Worcestershire sauce

4 ml (¾ tsp) ground coriander
pinch of salt
3 ml (½ tsp) sugar
dash of Tabasco
225 g (8 oz) ripe tomatoes

Trim the courgettes and slice them thinly. Peel the avocados and remove the stones. Slice the tomatoes in half, remove the seeds and chop them. Heat the chicken stock in a large saucepan, add the courgettes and simmer until tender but not mushy. Take the courgettes out of the saucepan with a slotted spoon and reserve the stock. Put the courgettes into a food processor with the peeled avocados and whizz until smooth. Add this purée to the cooking liquid in the saucepan, stir well, then mix in the yoghurt, lemon juice, Worcestershire sauce, coriander, salt, sugar and Tabasco. Heat thoroughly, stirring until everything is well blended, but do not boil. Serve garnished with the chopped tomatoes.

Avocado and zucchini soup

Parrot fish, red snapper, bream, tiger prawns, lobster, crab

FISH

Fish must be the world's most universal food. From Lake Titikaka, 5,000 metres (14,000 feet) up in the Andes, to the Jordan River Valley, below sea level, people fish, and cook and eat what they catch. In Japan they eat it raw, in Singapore they make a curry from just the heads, in New Orleans they cook it in envelopes, in Ecuador they soak it in sour orange juice, and in Cape Town they make a dish from the leftover legs of lobsters that someone else has eaten.

All over the world people love eating fish and it's not really surprising. While we survive on three or four main kinds of meat, with a little game thrown in for variety, there are literally hundreds of kinds of fish that are eaten, each with its own texture, flavour and subtleties. Some of the most exciting meals I've ever eaten were fish meals – an amazing Baked Pompano in a Vieux Carré restaurant in New Orleans; a spiced pomfret eaten in the tiny town of Cox's Bazaar, at the Burmese end of Bangladesh, in a vast empty pavilion of a restaurant that in the days of the Raj was full of sahibs and their families taking a beach holiday. It was served with deep-fried fingers of paratha that made chips seem forever superfluous. I remember a lobster crayfish eaten with peri peri sauce and drawn butter at the point in Africa where the Indian and Atlantic Oceans meet, a squid stuffed with coconut and spiced potato in Malaysia, spiced crab back in Jamaica, featherlight prawn balls in Hong Kong. I could go on, because fish is undoubtedly one of my passions. It's also usually very easy and very quick to cook. These days it is surprisingly easy to find quite exotic kinds of fish in Britain. I've seen shark in a Swindon supermarket and swordfish in Cardiff. A huge amount of exotic fish now comes into Billingsgate, the great London distributive fish market, every day. I've grouped the recipes into shellfish and conventional fish for convenience but most cuisines don't really pay much attention to that kind of division. Browse through the seafood selection I've set out below, make your choice and then stand by for a tastebud treat.

Shellfish

BUTTERFLY PRAWNS

Prawns come in all kinds of sizes and, across the world, all kinds of colours and flavours too. We have tended to regard quite small fish, about the size of a little finger at most, as standard prawns. But the Chinese, particularly the Cantonese in the southern part of China nearest Hong Kong, regard serious prawns as more the size of two thumbs put together – what we call Mediterranean prawns nowadays. This dish really requires quite large prawns though the giant ones aren't essential. You do need raw ones, and these can be found in most good fishmongers or Chinese shops.

12 large raw prawns (heads removed)
1 egg
100 g (4 oz) flour
150 ml (6 fl oz) water

Dipping Sauce
100 ml (4 fl oz) tomato passata
5 ml (1 tsp) soy sauce
5 ml (1 tsp) chilli garlic sauce
cooking oil

Take the shell off each prawn by splitting it down the back very carefully, leaving a hinge of flesh on the inside curve. When you have removed the shell you will see a thick black vein running down the back of the split prawn. Remove this and place each prawn cut side down, opened, on a firm surface. Using a thick frying pan base or the flat side of a cleaver, beat gently to loosen and spread each prawn so that it resembles a heart or butterfly shape. Do this with each of the prawns and put them in the fridge to chill. Meanwhile beat the egg, flour and water together to make a thin, light batter. Mix the sauce ingredients together and place in small bowls, one for each diner. Heat oil in a deep fryer until it is 180°C, 360°F. Dip each prawn individually into the batter, shake off the excess, and slide it carefully into the hot oil. Do not drop them in from a height. Allow each prawn to seal before adding the next. You may need to fry them in more than one batch depending on the size of your pan. After 2 minutes, shake or turn each prawn over so that they are cooked evenly on both sides. Cook for another 2–3 minutes, depending on the size of the prawns, until they are medium gold all over. Take out of the oil, allow to drain for a moment, and place onto crumpled kitchen paper to finish removing all the oil. Serve immediately on hot plates or bowls with the dipping sauce to season and flavour them. Eat them with fingers.

JAMBALAYA

Jambalaya is not just the name of a rather pleasant song recorded by The Carpenters, it is also the name given to a range of dishes eaten all over the southern states of America, particularly in Louisiana and the Cajun country. It is a dish of rice, vegetables and fish (and sometimes meat) that has great similarities to the Spanish *Paella* and may well have been influenced by the Spanish conquistadors who first colonized this part of the Americas from Europe. Jambalaya is a meal in a dish and can vary from cook to cook, day to day, and region to region. This version uses prawns as its main ingredient so it's important to realize that, on the Gulf of Mexico, prawns come the sort of size that eat cats, not the other way round. If you can buy some of the larger Tiger prawns that are now quite widely available in Britain, they are the ideal size for this recipe.

1 large onion, peeled and finely chopped
1 clove garlic, peeled and finely chooped
45 ml (3 tbs) cooking oil
1 green pepper, cut into 1 cm (¹/₂ in)
ribbons
4 stalks celery, trimmed and cut into 1 cm
(¹/₂ in) rounds

400 g (14 oz) tin Italian chopped tomatoes
5 ml (1 tsp) Tabasco or hot chilli sauce
5 ml (1 tsp) thyme
seasoning
225 g (8 oz) long grain rice
450 g (1 lb) raw large prawns, shelled
(or monkfish cut into prawn-sized pieces)

Fry the chopped onion and garlic gently in the oil. Add the pepper and celery to the vegetable mixture and fry for another 2 minutes. Put in the chopped tomatoes and the chilli and thyme; season and simmer for 20 minutes, partly covered. Measure the rice into a cup or measuring jug, and add that to the tomato mixture with twice its volume of water. Stir, bring to the boil, then turn the heat down and simmer for 10 minutes. Add the prawns (or fish), stir gently into the mixture and cook over the lowest possible heat for another 10 minutes, until the rice absorbs all the liquid and the prawns are cooked and pink. Tip into a serving bowl and decorate with parsley or chopped celery tops. It should have a
moist but not runny consistency.

ECUADORIAN SEVICHE OF SCALLOPS

Seviche is an Ecuadorian version of a style of cooking that exists all over central and northern South America. I really don't mean cooking in the traditional sense as this is a way of preparing fish without applying heat. The fish is 'cooked' in lime, lemon or bitter orange juice, marinating for up to 6 hours until the flesh has gone opaque, as though it had been steamed or fried. The flavour is not at all raw but surprisingly firm and succulent. In this recipe I suggest using scallops which are wonderful fish for cooking this way, but you can cook almost any firm, white-fleshed seafood in this style. Bass, mackerel, prawns, lobster and oysters are all commonly used and I think that monkfish or fresh hake would work very well too. Serve it on a bed of finely ribboned lettuce with a tomato and onion *salsa* sauce to season it.

6 fresh scallops
1 sweet onion, peeled and very thinly sliced
5 ml (1 tsp) salt

250 ml (½ pint) lemon, lime or bitter
(Seville) orange juice, or a mixture
30 ml (2 tbs) vegetable oil (not olive oil)

Remove the coral from the scallops and set aside. Slice each scallop across the grain into three pieces, then place with the coral in a glass or china bowl. Add the onion slices. Add the salt and citrus juices, making sure that they cover the fish, and leave to marinate, turning two or three times, for 4–6 hours. Remove the fish from the juice, and place on a bed of thinly sliced lettuce. Mix 30 ml (2 tbs) of the marinade with the oil and pour over the fish.

Salsa Sauce

2 medium tomatoes, skinned and finely
chopped

4 white spring onions, finely chopped
2 good shakes Tabasco sauce

Stir all the ingredients together and allow them to blend for up to 2 hours before using.

Ecuadorian seviche of scallops

Malaysian stuffed squid, gado gado

MALAYSIAN STUFFED SQUID

This recipe is really quite unexpected. It is unexpected because we tend to think of squid in this country as being cut into rings and deep fried or as an ingredient of a seafood salad. Here it is eaten whole. It is also unexpected because the stuffing of coconut and spiced potato is, to say the least, an unlikely marriage; and finally it is unexpected because it tastes devastatingly delicious. It's best eaten as part of a two- or three- dish Malaysian-type feast (see the Regional Meals section of page 7) but it also makes a nice light lunch served with a little Gado Gado salad (pages 157–8) and plain boiled rice. Ask your fishmonger to clean the squid for you but to leave the body whole. You can ask for the cleaned tentacles section if you like or you can just let him dispose of it for you. Connoisseurs think the tentacles are the best bit.

2 whole cleaned squid, approx 20–25 cm (8–10 in) long
1 bunch spring onions, trimmed and chopped
2.5 ml (½ tsp) each ground coriander and ground cumin
30 ml (2tbs) oil

450 g (1 lb) boiled potatoes
100 g (4 oz) grated coconut or 50 g (2 oz) desiccated coconut, soaked
15 ml (1tbs) soft brown sugar
30 ml (2 tbs) soy sauce
juice of a lemon

Wash the squid carefully, running water inside and out. Fry the chopped spring onion with the spices in the oil very gently for 2–3 minutes. Add the cooked potatoes, broken up with a fork into a rough mash. Fry together for 5 more minutes then stir in the grated or rehydrated coconut. Let the mixture cool a little before using it to stuff the squid. Lay in a small baking dish. Mix together the sugar, soy sauce and lemon juice and pour over the squid. Bake, covered loosely with foil, in a medium (180°C, 350°F, Gas mark 4) oven, for 20–25 minutes. Serve the squid sliced crosswise into 2.5 cm (1 in) rounds, with some of the sauce spooned over.

THAI RED PRAWN CURRY

Thai curries are very different from those you find on the Indian sub-continent. They come in three colours: red, orange and green, rather like traffic lights but, contrary to expectation, the degree of spicy heat of the curry goes in reverse order: red is the mildest, orange the next hottest and green the most explosive of all. This red curry can be eaten on its own with rice and a salad, but it is also traditionally eaten as one of four or five dishes that would be taken as a group family meal. As the main cooking is done in advance of adding the prawns you can use raw or cooked prawns in this case, simply giving the raw prawns about 5 minutes longer cooking.

15 ml (1 tbs) each ground red chilli powder, ground coriander, finely chopped garlic and Laos powder (see ingredients, page 6)
5 ml (1 tsp) each salt, grated lime peel, freshly ground black pepper
1 small onion, peeled and coarsely chopped
1 stalk lemon grass
60 ml (4 tbs) oil

225 g (8 oz) coconut cream dissolved in 250 ml (½ pint) hot water
5 ml (1 tsp) shrimp paste or anchovy paste (optional)
450 g (1 lb) shelled prawns
1 cucumber split lengthwise, with its seeds scooped out, and cut into 1 cm (½ in) half moons
chopped coriander leaves to garnish

Put the first five ingredient items into a food processor or liquidizer and grind together until a smooth paste is obtained. You may need to add a little water to help the blades work. Put the dissolved coconut cream into a wok or large saucepan and bring to the boil. Add the spice mixture and cook over a low heat, stirring, for about 10 minutes, until a film of oil appears around the edge of the dish and the spices give off their aroma. Add the shrimp or anchovy paste if you are using it, the prawns, and the cucumber. Cook gently for 3–4 minutes if the prawns are pre-cooked or for 10 minutes if they are raw. Stir the curry well, sprinkle with chopped coriander leaves and serve with rice.

Thai red prawn curry (top); Baked avocado with crab (bottom)

Cape Malay lobster leg curry, pilau rice, accompaniments

CAPE MALAY LOBSTER LEG CURRY

The Cape Malay people were brought to South Africa in the nineteenth century to act as personal servants, often as cooks, to the white colonists. They often came as indentured labour, but after serving their time many remained in the Cape and founded a vigorous sub-culture of their own. This curry was made from the legs of the plentiful and delicious Cape lobsters which were left over after the masters had eaten the succulent tails. Nowadays it's made with the tail of a lobster and just a few of the legs cracked open for tradition. It is normally served with yellow pilau rice (see page 167) and a range of condiments, including sliced bananas in lime juice, fresh grated coconut, mango chutney, and a carrot salad.

1–1.2 kg (2½ lb) lobster (you can also use crayfish or monkfish tails)
100 g (4 oz) coconut cream
2.5 cm (1 in) length fresh root ginger, peeled and finely chopped

2 large onions, peeled and chopped
1 clove garlic, peeled and finely chopped
salt
5 ml (1 tsp) brown sugar
5 ml (1 tsp) lemon or lime juice

15 ml (1 tbs) mild curry powder or 10 ml (2 tsp) turmeric and coriander, 5 ml (1 tsp) ground cumin, 2.5 ml (½ tsp) chilli powder, ground cinnamon and black pepper, and a pinch each of cloves and nutmeg, ground up and mixed together.

Boil the lobster in just enough water to cover it until it is thoroughly cooked (approximately 20 minutes). Allow to cool, split and remove the black vein which runs through the tail. Remove all the meat from the tail, the body, the claws if any, and at least 4 of the biggest legs, cracking them open to get the meat out. Cut into walnut-sized pieces where appropriate. If using monkfish or crayfish, cook in a similar way, then take the flesh from the bone or the shell and cut into cubes. Take a cupful of the strained water in which the lobster was cooked, and mix the coconut cream in it in a saucepan until it has melted. Add the spices and cook over a medium heat until a ring of oil appears in the dish and the spices smell cooked. Add the onions and garlic to the coconut cream spice mixture with another cup of water and cook for 15 minutes. Add the lobster meat. Season to taste with salt and let it heat through for 5 minutes over a low heat. Some cooks add a teaspoon each of brown sugar and lemon or lime juice at this point to balance the seasoning in the curry.

STIR-FRIED PRAWNS WITH SNOW PEAS

This is a South Chinese style of dish that looks extremely pretty as well as tasting delicious. It's very quick to make and is as much a favourite with people who 'don't like foreign food' as with those who have a taste for more exotic styles.

30 ml (2 tbs) cooking oil
1 clove garlic, peeled and finely chopped
1 cm (½ in) piece fresh root ginger, peeled and finely chopped
350 g (12 oz) peeled raw prawns
white section of 8 spring onions, trimmed and cut into 5 cm (2 in) lengths

225 g (8 oz) snow peas (mangetout), topped and tailed
15 ml (1 tbs) soy sauce
10 ml (2 tsp) cornflour
15 ml (1 tbs) lemon juice
5 ml (1 tsp) brown sugar

Heat the oil in a wok or large saucepan, then add the ginger and garlic and fry for half a minute. Add the prawns and fry, stirring regularly, for 3–4 minutes until they change colour. Add the spring onions and the snow peas. Stir-fry the mixture for 2 minutes. Mix together the soy sauce, cornflour, lemon juice, brown sugar and enough water to produce a liquid the thickness of single cream. Pour this onto the prawn mixture and bring to a rapid boil, stirring all the time. The sauce will thicken and go glossy: as soon as it does, the dish is ready.

JAMAICA CRAB BACK

Although I first encountered this dish in Jamaica, it is common in slightly varied forms all over the West Indies. It's made with what are called land crabs, crabs that live on the edge of the sea, often in the mangrove thickets, and spend a good deal of their time at night on land, hunting. The people who like baked crab spend a good deal of the night hunting the crabs in turn, using bright lights, sticks and large sacks. A crab hunt is a source of great excitement and often the crabs would be caught in their hundreds. They are, I am told, more scarce now. English marine crabs make a very satisfactory substitute, although they are significantly larger and moister than their Caribbean cousins. An English crab should feed two, whereas in the West Indies you would need a crab per person. This dish makes a wonderful first course.

2 cooked crabs, weighing about 500 g (1 lb)
each
1 bunch spring onions, trimmed and
chopped
5 ml (1 tsp) chilli sauce

pinch thyme
50 g (2 oz) butter
100 g (4 oz) fresh breadcrumbs
seasoning

Remove the meat from the crab, mixing the brown and white together (or get your fishmonger to do it for you). Mix the spring onion and thyme with the crab meat and the chilli sauce. Melt the butter, stir in the breadcrumbs, and allow to cool. Add half the breadcrumb mixture to the crab meat, season the mixture and pack it back into the cleaned, oiled shells. Cover with the remaining breadcrumbs. Bake in a medium to high oven (190°C, 375°F, Gas Mark 5) until they are brown, approximately 10–15 minutes. Don't let them dry out.

BAKED AVOCADO WITH CRAB

We tend to think of avocados as essentially salad ingredients to eat cold but in the land of their development, the highlands of Central America, they were often, and still are, eaten hot. It's important to get avocados at the right point for successful cooking; when they are ripe enough to give slightly to the touch but not in any sense squelchy or discoloured, because if they are they will collapse while heating. This particular recipe, including crab, comes from the north coast of South America that runs along between Venezuela and the Guyanas.

2 large avocados, ripe but not squelchy
175 g (6 oz) cooked crab meat, white
3 spring onions
60 ml (4 tbs) mayonnaise

5 ml (1 tsp) dried red pepper flakes (or
salad seasoning which includes red pepper
flakes
juice of 1 lemon

Split the avocado and remove the stone. Rub the avocado with the cut side of the lemon to stop it going brown. Finely chop the onions. Mix together the onions, crab, mayonnaise and the dried red pepper flakes. Put half the lemon juice over the avocado and the remaining juice on the crab. Fill the dent of each avocado with a mound of the crab mixture. Cover with a butter paper or oiled greaseproof paper or foil and put into the oven, 375°F/190°C/170C Fan/Gas 5/ middle of the Aga roasting oven, for 15 minutes or until the avocados and filling are hot but not soggy. It could take up to 20 minutes depending on the size of the fruit.

Conventional Fish

TANDOORI SPICED TROUT

There is a great tradition in Indian cookery for very simple food, rubbed with spices and either grilled or baked. This is essentially an outdoor style of cooking used a lot by people for picnics or when out hunting or fishing and it hasn't reached the high street Indian restaurant yet. Tandoori cooking is a slightly more sophisticated version of this kind of cooking, involving marinating the fish or meat in spiced yoghurt and then baking it. That's the technique I'm going to suggest for one of our more delicate fishes, trout. Although India is usually portrayed as a great arid country, it has an enormous number of rivers, lakes and tanks (huge artificial reservoirs built to supply houses or areas) and in almost all of them there are a horde of different species of fish. Some of them are more highly prized than others but the most valued fish for culinary purposes in India all come from the great rivers. It's entirely appropriate therefore to cook trout in tandoori style. The delicate spicing and marinading goes very well either with the brown trout or the far more widely available rainbow trout. Eat this with some of the Indian breads on pages 171–8 and the cucumber raita on page 225.

10 ml (2 tsp) ground coriander
5 ml (1 tsp) ground cumin
5 ml (1 tsp) turmeric powder
2.5 ml (½ tsp) ground ginger
2.5 ml (½ tsp) garlic salt

2.5 ml (½ tsp) chilli powder
5 ml (1 tsp) paprika
250 ml (½ pint) plain yoghurt
4 small trout, weighing approximately
150–225 g (6–8 oz), cleaned

Mix all the spices with the yoghurt and spoon over the trout, making sure that some paste goes into the cavities. Leave to marinate for at least 4 hours, preferably 6, turning at least once during this process. Heat the oven to medium hot (200°C, 400°F, Gas mark 6). Remove the trout from the marinade and allow to drain a little, then place on a rack in a baking dish. Place the dish in the oven and bake for 20 minutes, then turn and bake for another 10 minutes. Do not baste during this time as it should be dry when finished. Serve on a bed of finely shredded lettuce with a lemon quarter for each person to squeeze over the fish.

Baked snapper

BAKED SNAPPER

Snapper is a favourite tropical fish the world over. Snappers are now widely available in Britain, especially at fish shops with a clientele from the West Indies or the spice islands of the Indian Ocean. It is a fish which benefits from being baked whole. It's quite difficult to fillet when raw but when it's cooked the very solid flesh lifts easily off the bones. A fish weighing 1–1½ kg/2–3 lb will easily feed four people. It needs to be eaten with rice and a salad or perhaps just with crusty bread and the salad served afterwards.

1 large snapper, cleaned
5 ml (1 tsp) salt
60 ml (4tbs) oil
1 red chilli pepper, finely chopped

2 limes
a bouquet of herbs made up of thyme, bay leaf and celery leaf

Wash the fish inside and out and rub with a little salt. Take a piece of foil large enough to wrap around the fish loosely and use half the oil to grease it. Mix the rest of the oil with the chopped chilli. Slice one of the limes thinly and lay a line of lime slices down the foil. Lay the fish on this, and place the remaining lime slices on top of the fish. Stuff the cavity with the herbs. Squeeze the other lime over the fish and spread the chilli and oil mixture on one side only. Fold the foil together to form an airtight package without clamping it down tightly on the fish, and bake in a medium oven (180°C, 350°F, Gas mark 4) for 55–60 minutes until the fish is cooked right through. Carefully pour the juices from the foil out into a warmed jug, for diners to help themselves. Use them discreetly because they will be strongly flavoured with the chilli.

ESCOVITCH FISH

The word *escovitch* is Spanish and means 'preserved in vinegar', one of the few methods available in the days before refrigeration. It's still a soused style but these days the purpose isn't preservation but flavour. There are many variations of escovitch dishes throughout the West Indies but my favourite is the one made with small fish, weighing about 150–225 g (6–8 oz) each. In the Caribbean parrot fish are often used, with their vividly coloured scales and remarkably matching coloured bones: blue, turquoise, red and bright green. They are beginning to be imported quite widely (and not too expensively) into this country from various tropical seas. Ask your fishmonger to see if he can get parrot fish; if not, use mackerel, or cutlets of hake or rock salmon.

700 g (1½ lb) individual fish (4) cleaned, or
450 g (1 lb) fish cutlets
60 ml (4 tbs) cooking oil
1 onion, peeled and thinly sliced
1 carrot, peeled and thinly sliced
1 stick celery, trimmed and thinly sliced

2 small red or green chilli peppers
sprig of thyme
salt and pepper
225 ml (8 fl oz) vinegar – cane, cider or
white wine

Rinse and dry the fish and fry it in the oil till golden brown and fully cooked. Place the onion, carrot and celery slices with all the other ingredients in the vinegar and bring to the boil in a pan. When the fish has been fried, place it in a serving dish with raised sides and pour over it the hot vinegar. Leave to marinate for 6–24 hours. To serve, a piece of fish is garnished with a few slices of onion, carrot and celery and served with a tablespoon of the sauce. It makes a superb first course or part of a larger buffet with a variety of other dishes.

*Escovitch fish – frying the parrot fish; Escovitch fish served with onion,
carrot and celery*

SALMON TERRIAKI

The Japanese eat more fish per head of the population than any other nation on earth. The great fish market in Tokyo is the biggest and best in the world. When I visited it I was told that it handled more than £10,000,000 worth of fish every day. The tuna sales section alone was spread out over an area the size of two football pitches. Tuna is king in Japan. But for the terriaki style of cooking, in a sweet and soy glaze, salmon is the favourite fish. Although the Japanese cut the fish slightly differently to the way we do in this country, salmon cutlets are ideal for this dish. Salmon Terriaki is good served with a little miso soup (see page 17), white rice and a cucumber salad which can be dressed either with a European-style vinaigrette or a little sugar, water and vinegar mixed together in the Japanese style.

100 ml (4 fl oz) shoyu sauce (Japanese-style soy sauce, see Ingredients, page 6)
30 ml (2 tbs) white sugar
30 ml (2 tbs) apple juice (properly Mirin, a sweetened rice wine, see Ingredients page 6)

30 ml (2 tbs) frying oil
4 salmon cutlets, weighing about 100 g (4 oz) each

Mix the shoyu sauce with the sugar and the apple juice or Mirin and combine it with an equivalent volume of water. Stir till the sugar is dissolved. Heat a frying-pan (non-stick is a good idea) and add the oil then fry the salmon cutlets gently on both sides until the flesh goes opaque. Pour in the sauce mixture and bring to the boil. Boil for 2 minutes then turn the salmon carefully and boil for another 2 minutes. Put the salmon on to warmed serving plates and continue boiling the sauce until it has a syrupy texture, which should take about 2 minutes. Pour over the salmon.

SASHIMI

Continuing the Japanese theme, here is the simple form of their famous raw fish hors d'oeuvre. Before you dismiss the idea, remember that when we eat oysters or smoked salmon we are eating raw fish too, so the idea isn't really that peculiar. It is, however, essential that the fish is stunningly fresh. After my recent trip to Japan I tried to make Sashimi with fish bought at a local supermarket and it tasted terrible. You must have fish that your fishmonger (or your fish catcher) assures you is almost straight out of water. I've suggested mackerel, salmon and sole, but in Japan they eat almost any fish in this style and fresh tuna is the absolute favourite. The important thing is to cut it in extremely small, thin slices; eaten like this, it is extremely filling, so you don't need a lot. Arrange the slices as prettily as you can on plates that have some kind of oriental or willow pattern design. Don't omit the traditional garnish of grated radish and the shoyu sauce dip as these make all the difference.

100 g (4 oz) each of salmon fillet, sole fillet and mackerel fillet, skinned
5 cm (2 in) length of daikon, peeled (giant white radish, also known as mooli)

5 ml (1 tsp) made mustard (preferably Wasabi Japanese Green horseradish)
juice of a lemon
120 ml (8 tbs) shoyu sauce

Lay each fish fillet out on a cutting board in turn and slice across the grain into thin, neat slices using the sharpest knife you have. Arrange each fish on an individual plate, in an overlapping pattern, leaving space in the middle. Grate the radish carefully into long strands, and pile those strands in the middle of each plate. Decorate with a few leaves of parsley, spring onion or coriander if you wish. Mix the mustard, the lemon juice and the shoyu sauce together and pour into individual small bowls for each diner. To eat: pick up a piece of fish, preferably with chopsticks, dip it in the sauce, and eat it, one piece at a time, taking a pinch of the very mild radish to refresh the palate between flavours.

SALT GRILLED FISH

Another Japanese style with fish shows the variety of techniques and the interesting flavours that can be achieved with very simple methods. This is an old fashioned way of cooking fish in Japan with a history going back a thousand or more years. It produces a very delicate result which is surprisingly unsalty. You can use herring, sardines or mackerel for this recipe. In Japan they would use a species of mackerel known as Horse Mackerel, with a large head and succulent flesh.

4 herrings (or small mackerel), weighing about 150 g (6 oz) each, cleaned
60 ml (4 tbs) coarse salt

4 long bamboo or metal skewers (2.5 cm/1 in longer than the fish)

Wash the gutted and cleaned fish under cold running water and pat dry with kitchen towels. Rub a tablespoon of salt into and over each fish and leave them on a plate or rack to drain for at least 30 minutes. Sprinkle a little more salt over them if all that you put on them in the first place has dissolved. Push a skewer through each fish from the mouth end through to the tail to keep them absolutely straight while grilling. Pre-heat the grill and grill for 10 minutes, turning at least twice. Make sure the fish along the back flakes easily before serving with rice and one or two vegetable dishes, and perhaps some miso soup (page 17).

VIEUX CARRÉ POMPANO

I first had this dish in a tiny restaurant in the Vieux Carré quarter of New Orleans, long before Creole or Cajun cooking was fashionable. It uses the luxury fish of the Gulf of Mexico, the Pompano. You can buy it occasionally in this country but it's fairly hard to come by, so I suggest you try a fillet of brill or a piece of the chicken halibut that is often in our shops from Greenland waters. The dish is cooked *en papillote* which originally means 'in an envelope'. You can, if you like, make an envelope out of greaseproof paper that's been carefully oiled, but I think it's much easier to use a double thickness of tin foil. The important thing is not to seal the foil tightly against the fish but to leave an air space in which it can cook and allow the flavours to mingle. Don't open the individual parcels before serving, as one of the diner's pleasures is to open his or her piece of fish and have the wonderful combination of scents waft out. I think this is best served on its own with a vegetable or salad to follow.

4 large rectangular pieces aluminium
cooking foil
60 ml (4 tbs) cooking oil (not olive)
4 fillets fish (see above), each weighing
about 150–225 g (6–8 oz)
half a red and half a green pepper, finely
chopped

1 bunch spring onions, trimmed and finely
chopped
225 g (8 oz) peeled prawns
2.5 ml (½ tsp) each fresh thyme, tarragon
and oregano, chopped
4 ripe tomatoes, chopped
2 limes
seasoning

Oil the foil pieces carefully and place a fillet of fish in the middle of each oblong. Fry the chopped peppers, spring onions and tomatoes in the remaining oil for 2 minutes, until softened. Spread on top of the fillets of fish, layer over equal portions of prawns and sprinkle the mixed herbs on the top. Cut the limes in half and squeeze the juice of half a lime onto each fillet of fish. Season with salt and a little pepper and fold the foil carefully around the fish, leaving an air space for the flavours to mingle above the fish fillet. Place carefully on a baking tray and bake for 25–30 minutes in a hot oven (200°C, 400°F, Gas mark 6). Serve carefully on to plates and open in front of each diner.

VERA CRUZ FISH BAKE

Vera Cruz is a large town in Mexico and the simple but delicious style of cooking fish that is supposed to derive from there is enormously popular across the whole of the country. As with all such popular dishes, though, it varies in detail from place to place and from cook to cook. The fish usually used in Mexico is bass but any firm fish like brill, haddock or bream will do very well. You need fillets, not cutlets. The key ingredient in the recipe is the flavouring of capers and olives, with some chilli to spike it. I've given the basic Mexican-style recipe here but you can, if you like, add chopped red and green peppers to the sauce as well.

225 g (8 oz) onions, peeled and finely sliced
2 cloves garlic, peeled and finely sliced
225 g (8 oz) tomatoes, chopped (tinned Italian tomatoes, drained, can be used)
60 ml (4 tbs oil)

30 ml (2 tbs) capers
15–20 stuffed green olives (with pimento stuffing)
1 fresh green chilli, de-seeded and cut into thin strips
700 g (1½ lb) fish fillets (see above)
seasoning

Fry the onions, garlic and chopped tomatoes in the oil, adding a little water if necessary, and cook until the mixture is thoroughly soft. Add the capers, olives and chilli. Mix thoroughly and pour into a baking dish. Lay the fish fillets on top, season, and cover with butter papers or foil. Bake for 25 minutes in a medium oven (180°C, 350°F, Gas mark 4), until the fish is cooked. Traditionally this is served with new potatoes and surrounded by triangles of bread fried crisp in butter.

FISH FILLETS IN PRAWN AND VEGETABLE SAUCE

In Brazil prawns are often used as a flavouring, as much as an ingredient in their own right. Both fresh and dried prawns are used in this way and this dish, from the Bahai area of Brazil, uses them as a basis to create a very decorative red, pink and green sauce on fish. You can use any firm fish for this dish although in Brazil it tends to be one of the tropical variety.

2 fish fillets (rock, salmon, huss or cod)
1 onion
1 medum sized clove of garlic
1 can tinned tomatoes
30–45 g (2–3 tbsp) oil (corn or sunflower)
100 g (4 oz) peeled prawns

5 ml (1 tsp) chilli sauce
fresh coriander or parsley
5 ml (1 tsp) sugar
salt and pepper
rice to serve

Fry the chopped onion, tinned tomatoes and chopped garlic until they form a rich sauce which is quite thick. Add the chilli sauce and sugar. Finely chop the prawns or put them in a blender, the do not need to be puréed but they should be very finely chopped. In a frying pan place the fish fillets on top of the sauce and the prawns on top of that. Cook, covered for 8–10 minutes or until the fish is cooked right through. When cooked the fish should flake with a fork. Sprinkle with parsley or coriander to taste and pour some of the sauce over the fish. Serve with rice.

Ginger baked kingfish

GINGER BAKED KINGFISH

This is the second of the recipes from Gemma's restaurant in a tree on the Caribbean in Tobago. She uses a well known Caribbean fish called Kingfish, but any large firm white fish like cod or haddock will do. Occasionally you can find kingfish in fishmongers that specialise in serving the Caribbean community but what makes this special is the sauce, a West Indian version of sweet and sour, heavily flavoured with ginger.

700 g (1½ lb) firm white fish in cutlets
100 g (4 oz) plain flour
2.5 ml (½ tsp) each powdered bay leaf, paprika, salt and pepper
60 ml (4 tbs) sunflower or peanut oil
25 g (1 oz) peeled and crushed ginger (or use jar)
225 g (8 fl oz) pineapple juice

1 red and 1 green pepper
6 spring onions
15 ml (1 tbs) each vinegar and sugar
15 ml (1 tbs) soy sauce
1 clove of garlic
30 ml (2 tbs) cornflour

Mix the salt, pepper, paprika and bay leaf into the plain flour. Put it into a plastic bag and add the fish cutlets, sealing the bag and shaking to make sure they are completely covered. Shallow fry them in a couple of tablespoons of the oil until golden on all sides, about 8 minutes. Meanwhile, peel, clean and shred the spring onions and the red and green pepper and fine chop the garlic. Sauté the pepper, onion, garlic and ginger together in the remaining oil for 3 minutes. Add the pineapple juice and the soy sauce and simmer for 10 minutes. Mix the cornflour with a little water and stir it into the sauce, bringing it gently back to the boil until the sauce thickens. Drain the fish on kitchen paper and pour the sauce over it before serving.

ZANZIBAR FISH CURRY

The little island of Zanzibar is famous for its cloves and in past centuries was notorious for its part in the slave trade. What the many visitors and traders who came to the island brought, however, was a wide range of dishes and methods of cooking. Many of these crossed over to the mainland of Africa and into the culinary repertoire of Tanzania, the country that's an amalgam of the old Tanganyika and Zanzibar. This dish is an African or even perhaps Arab curry. On the island itself it's known as 'Samaki wa nazi' and is normally eaten with plain boiled rice.

700 g (1½ lb) firm fish (English equivalents: haddock, rock salmon, monk fish)
225 g (8 oz) onions
2 cloves of garlic
1 level dessertspoon curry powder (shop bought or see Ingredients page 5)
1 fresh red chilli (or 1 tsp fresh crushed chilli)

1 tin coconut cream
50 ml (2 fl oz) peanut or sunflower oil
30 ml (2 tbsp) tomato purée
juice of 1 lime
salt and pepper

As much as is possible, skin and bone the fish (or get your fishmonger to do it for you) and cut into 8 even sized pieces. Heat the oil in a saucepan and fry the fish gently in that until lightly gold (3 minutes each side). Season generously with the salt and pepper and remove to a warm plate. In the same pan, put the finely chopped onion and garlic and fry until transparent. Add the curry powder, the de-seeded chopped chilli and the coconut milk. Cook gently, stirring, for about 10 minutes until the spices form a thin layer on top of the coconut milk. Add the fish back in and the juice of the lime. Stir, heat, and check for seasoning.

Vieux Carré pompano (top); Bang bang chicken (bottom)

CHICKEN AND OTHER POULTRY

I have a vivid and now rather sad memory of an extraordinary meal eaten in the Lebanese mountains one winter, just before chaos descended on that part of the Middle East. We had been visiting a beautiful ancient palace, it was after lunchtime and we were ravenous. Our driver found a café which was clearly closed for the season but he persuaded them to open for us, and a lady disappeared into the garden with a determined look on her face and a hatchet in her hand. Forty-five minutes later we were served with a simple but exquisite meal of Farouj Meshwi, or grilled chicken, in a style that in Britain would be called spatch-cocked – split along the backbone, beaten flat with the side of a cleaver and grilled over a fierce heat. Served with it was a simple flat bread, a salad of bitter green leaves dressed with olive oil and lemon juice, and a bowl containing what at first looked like slightly lumpy cream but which turned out to be fresh garlic crushed with salt, of an incredible pungency and flavour. We shared the chicken, which was dipped into the garlic, wrapped in bread, and consumed almost instantaneously. It was one of the greatest chicken dinners I have ever eaten, and an example of how delicious the simplest ingredients can be when they're cooked freshly and with skill.

Many other happy memories of meals seem to feature chicken, perhaps because it is the most universal of all meats. I have memories of earth-floored kitchens in India which produced exquisite confections of chicken, almonds and cream; of spiced fried chicken eaten at Easter in a tiny, green valley on the Mexico-California border; of chicken fricassée eaten in the high mountains of Jamaica; Cantonese-style chicken with its sweet and sour flavours in Hong Kong; and further down the coastline of South East Asia, mouth-searingly hot chicken in chilli in Singapore.

The number of chicken dishes is endless and their flavours as varied as the countries and the people who cook them. Chicken seems to have a unique gift for carrying flavour and nuance from the other ingredients that are cooked with it. What I've chosen here are a number of my absolute favourite dishes. Some of them are strongly regional in style, like the Chicken Korma that should be eaten as part of an Indian meal, or the Kung Po Chicken that's best served with other dishes from China; and some can be eaten in their own right or as part of an everyday meal, like the Malaysian Crisp Garlic Chicken or the Jamaican Chicken Fricassée. Some are simple, and one or two are more complicated, but I think you'll find that all of them are worth the cooking.

Chicken isn't the only poultry eaten in exotic lands, of course. In fact, some of the most famous dishes in the world are based on other poultry. Peking Duck is the prime example. In Afghanistan, Iran, and the southern provinces of Russia, Fasanjan, a dish of pheasant in a walnut sauce with pomegranate as a flavouring, has equal fame. Spiced quail is a legendary dish amongst hunters in India, especially when eaten around the fireside at the end of a day's hunting. I've given recipes for all these dishes, not forgetting Mole Poblano, the national dish of Mexico, which is turkey in a rich chocolatey sauce.

A Jamaican spread – Chicken fricassée, avocado salad, fried plantains, baked sweet potatoes rice and peas

BANG BANG CHICKEN FROM SZECHWAN

This cold chicken dish comes from Szechwan, the most westerly province of China. It's an extraordinary dish, simple to make, with very strong and vivid flavours typical of Szechwanese cooking. I came across it in the first of the Szechwanese restaurants to open in London. It's served in China as a first course, what Kenneth Lo said the Chinese call a 'wine drinking dish', something to get the party warmed up. It makes a wonderful first course for a very grand meal or a splendid main course for a summer supper, especially on a warm evening.

1 medium-sized chicken
a piece of lemon rind
2 bay leaves
2 cucumbers, washed
1 crisp head of lettuce
60 ml (4 tbs) peanut butter

30 ml (2 tbs) sesame oil
5 ml (1 tsp) each sugar and salt
½ cup water
15 ml (1 tbs) chilli oil (or 5 ml/1 tsp
Tabasco mixed with 15 ml/1 tbs cooking
oil)

Clean and trim the chicken and poach it for 45 minutes in just enough water to cover, with the lemon rind and bay leaves. Allow it to cool, keeping the liquid which is very good chicken stock. Skin the chicken and take the meat off the bones. Cut into 5 mm (¼ in) slices across the grain. Shred the cucumbers on a mandolin or through a food processor, or with a sharp knife if you prefer – it should be in shreds about the length of 2 or 3 matchsticks. Wash and dry the lettuce and cut that into very fine ribbons. Mix all the remaining sauce ingredients together in a saucepan and heat gently. You can replace the water with some of the chicken stock if you prefer. When it comes to the boil you will find that the sauce thickens and becomes smooth and shiny. Take it off the heat and allow it to cool a little. Arrange the lettuce as a bed on a large serving plate, scatter the shredded cucumber over it, and place the chicken on top of that. Dribble a little of the sauce from a spoon over the chicken and serve with an extra bowl of sauce for diners to add if they choose. The sauce is pretty fierce but its nutty flavour perfectly complements the salad and chicken.

MALAYSIAN CRISPY GARLIC CHICKEN

This dish is typical of the way that chicken's cooked all over South East Asia. In Malaysia, on the Island of Penang, there are a couple of marvellous open-air food markets, or hawker markets as they're called. They're quite substantial in the daytime but in the evening the stalls stretch for more than a mile along the roads bordering the beaches and the sea. The most extraordinary range of foods can be eaten there, from dried squid rolled out through a mangle to be heated briefly over charcoal and rolled up again into a tube to be eaten, to exotic and complicated soups, noodle dishes and, not least, this marvellous garlic-flavoured crisp chicken. It's normally served with a small cup of soup made from the chicken bones, some spring onions and a little rice on the side.

1 chicken, jointed into 8 pieces with the bony bits of the carcass removed (these can be made into the soup that's traditionally drunk with it)
6 cloves garlic, peeled

7.5 ml (1½ tsp) salt
1 small fresh chilli pepper, halved, de-seeded and chopped
juice of half a lemon
oil for deep frying

Trim the chicken joints and put them in a bowl. Crush the garlic cloves with the salt and the chilli pepper. You can either do this with the point of a sharp knife or put into a small food processor or liquidizer. Add the lemon juice to help the blades work. Spread the garlic, salt, chilli and lemon mixture over the pieces of chicken and leave them to marinate for at least 4 hours. If you wish, you can cut small gashes in the chicken flesh in order to allow the flavour to penetrate further. Heat the oil till it's just below smoking point (190°C, 380°F if you've got a deep fryer with a thermostat). Put the chicken pieces into a basket and lower it quickly into the hot oil. Turn the heat down to 170°C/340°F or turn the flame down if you're using a pan on the stove. Allow to cook for 10 minutes, then turn carefully and cook for at least 5 minutes more. The skin should be medium to dark brown and crispy, while the inside of the chicken should be succulent and tender. The garlic coating will have fried to a crisp paste and will add crunch as well as flavour to the delicious morsels of chicken.

Chicken tikka (top); Chicken with mango (bottom)

CHICKEN TIKKA

Chicken Tikka is essentially pieces of chicken marinated in a little yoghurt and spices, put on a skewer and either grilled or baked. This is the most common way that chicken is eaten in Pakistan and the northern parts of India, deriving from the traditions of nomadic cooking, where food was cooked very simply in the open air over charcoal or wood fires. This outdoor method of cooking has been refined, particularly in the Punjab area near Delhi where tandoori cooking developed, and has recently achieved enormous popularity, both in India and abroad. Chicken Tikka can be cooked with the bone in or out, it can be marinated for a long time or quite briefly, and it can be eaten with rice or any of the many wonderful Indian breads for which you'll find recipes on pages 171–8. A salad of yoghurt and sliced cucumber and tomato is delicious with it. It is traditionally eaten with the fingers.

1 onion, peeled and finely sliced
juice of a lemon
225 ml (8 fl oz) natural yoghurt
1 clove garlic, crushed
5 ml (1 tsp) salt
10 ml (1 dsp) each ground coriander and turmeric

5 ml (1 tsp) each ground ginger and paprika
2.5 ml (½ tsp) each chilli powder and ground black pepper
700 g (1½ lb) chicken pieces (legs, thighs or breasts will do)
lemon quarters to serve

Add the onion slices, and lemon juice to the yoghurt, with the garlic, salt and spices. Mix thoroughly. Leave chicken legs whole, cut thighs across the bone, and divide breasts into two. Marinate the chicken pieces in the yoghurt for a minimum of 2 hours and up to 24 hours if kept in the fridge. Turn the pieces of meat from time to time to make sure they're evenly coated. Remove the chicken from the marinade, and thread the pieces onto skewers. Cook them in a very hot oven (210°C, 425°F, Gas mark 7) for 30 minutes, or if grilling them, under a pre-heated grill for 10 minutes a side. The chicken is meant to be crisp on the outside and cooked through at the centre. Do not baste or attempt to save the juices that drip from it. It should be served when cooked on a bed of shredded lettuce with lemon quarters and with either plain boiled rice or hot parathas or chapatis.

CHICKEN TIKKA MASALA

This is really a way of using up leftover Chicken Tikka. You may feel this is unlikely once you have tasted it, but if you do have any left over or if you fancy making a double portion in order to make the second dish a couple of days later, it is well worth it. Although the basis is the same, the way the Chicken Tikka Masala is presented is very different. In certain places this dish is known as Chicken Tikka Karai, which means it's been cooked in a Karai, a kind of mini black-iron wok much used in the north-west frontier provinces of India. The finished dish has a bright, clear taste to it that's often missing in Indian food. It's nice served with rice and perhaps some vegetable curries.

450 g (1 lb) cooked chicken tikka (see previous recipe)
30 ml (2 tbs) oil or ghee
1 large onion, peeled and finely sliced
1 red and 1 green pepper, cut in half, de-seeded and finely sliced
2 large ripe tomatoes, skinned and quartered

10 ml (1 dsp) garam masala (see Ingredients, page 5)
5 ml (1 tsp) soft brown sugar
juice of half a lemon
salt
lemon quarters to serve

Cut the cooked chicken into walnut-sized pieces without any bone. Heat the oil or ghee in a medium-sized frying pan and fry the onion with the peppers until soft. Add the chicken pieces and cook over a high heat until the whole mixture is heated through. Add the tomato quarters and squash them down to expel a little juice. Cover the pan and cook for 2 minutes. Stir in the garam masala, sugar and lemon juice, and check for seasoning – it may need a little salt, but won't need any pepper. Serve sizzling hot with a quarter of lemon for each diner.

Chicken tikka masala

CHICKEN KORMA

Chicken Korma is one of the great and luxurious treats. It was a dish brought to its height at the Mogul courts, which flourished in India from the sixteenth to the eighteenth century and where Indian food reached a height of refinement not since matched. It's a mild form of what we call curry and is made to a number of different recipes all over the Indian sub-continent. My favourite version, which I think is probably closest to the original, is made with almonds and slightly soured or yoghurted cream. It uses whole rather than ground spices which, surprisingly, provide a really strong flavour that is nevertheless much more subtle than the ground-spiced versions of the dish that I've eaten.

Chicken Korma is best served with pilau rice (see page 167), as one of two or three dishes in a special or family dinner party meal. I think that the Bhuna Ghosht (page 104) and the Lemon Sag (pages 144–5) would make, with the pilau, a really wonderful meal for six to eight people.

4 chicken breasts (part boned)
2.5 cm (1 in) piece fresh root ginger, peeled
and finely chopped
1 clove garlic, peeled and crushed
125 ml (5 fl oz) plain yoghurt
5 ml (1 tsp) salt
2 bay leaves

cinnamon stick
6 cardamom pods
4 cloves
6 peppercorns
1 small chilli pepper
450 g (1 lb) onions, peeled and sliced
60 ml (4 tbs) ghee or cooking oil
50 g (2 oz) ground almonds

Cut the chicken in half across the breast. Mix the ginger and garlic with half the yoghurt and the salt. Rub over the chicken pieces, then place them in a shallow dish with the bay leaves, cinnamon, cardamom, cloves, peppercorns and chilli pepper and leave to stand for 30 minutes to 8 hours. Fry the onions in ghee or oil until they're golden brown. Add the meat and yoghurt and spice mixture to the pan, then add water till it comes to within 1 cm (½ in) of the top of the chicken. Cook quickly, spooning the sauce over the chicken from time to time and turning the chicken halfway through. The liquid should pretty well evaporate. Mix the ground almonds with the remaining yoghurt and a cupful of water. Stir to make sure it's smooth and add to the chicken mixture. Heat through gently until the mixture simmers. Add a squeeze of lemon and a little sugar to the sauce if you like, before serving.

CHICKEN FRICASSÉE

This is the national dish of Jamaica, served with the rice and peas you will find on page 168. It used to be served as a special treat on Sundays before battery chickens arrived on that island in the sun. But even if you aren't using what used to be called a country fowl, this method of cooking does produce a most delicious dish, somewhere between a sauté and a casserole. I can remember eating it at different times all over Jamaica but perhaps the most memorable time was my first trip up into the mountains to the town of Newcastle, which used to be a British military post; it is so high, at over 1,600 m (5,000 ft), that the climate changes. For the first time after weeks of a heatwave I felt cool and refreshed, and my first Chicken Fricassée put the crown on a really terrific day. As well as the rice and peas, this is eaten with fried slices of plantain, a kind of giant cooking banana which is peeled, cut into 1 cm (½ in) slices across the grain, floured and fried, and also a green salad with avocado slices mixed in. If you can't find fresh red chilli peppers for the spiciness, I suggest you use a few drops of Tabasco or Jamaica chilli sauce instead.

1 large chicken, jointed into 8 pieces
juice of a lime
1 large onion, peeled and finely chopped
2 cloves garlic, peeled and finely chopped

225 g (8 oz) tomatoes, chopped
1 red chilli pepper, de-seeded and chopped
1 sprig fresh thyme or 5 ml (1 tsp) dried
60 ml (4 tbs) oil

Squeeze the lime juice over the chicken pieces, making sure all the joints get a good coating. Put the onions, garlic, tomatoes, chilli and thyme in a shallow dish and put the chicken pieces to marinate in the mixture for at least 30 minutes. Take the chicken out of the bowl. Heat the oil in a frying pan into which all the chicken pieces will fit flat, then fry them until they're well browned. Pour in the marinade mixture and add enough water so that the chicken is half immersed. Cover the pan and simmer for 20 minutes, then turn the chicken pieces and simmer for another 10 minutes. Season generously and serve with the sauce poured over the chicken in a serving dish. It will have thickened and reduced and taken on a delicious herby flavour while cooking.

KUNGPAO CHICKEN

Legend has it that this chicken dish was the favourite of a governor of Szechwan province in the seventeenth and eighteenth centuries. Like most Szechwanese dishes, this one is quite spicy on the palate. It goes very well as part of a Szechwanese meal, perhaps to follow the Bang Bang Chicken on page 58. It's essentially a stir fry dish and therefore you can prepare most of the ingredients in advance and cook it at the last minute when you're ready. It's designed to be eaten with plain, boiled rice, to absorb all the delicious sauce.

450 g (1 lb) boneless chicken breasts
15 ml (3 tsp) cornflour
1 egg white
30 ml (2 tbs) oil
1 clove garlic, peeled and finely chopped
1 cm (½ in) piece fresh root ginger, peeled and finely chopped
2–4 dried red chillis (depending on taste)

3 spring onions, trimmed and cut into thin rounds
30 ml (2 tbs) tangerine or orange juice
30 ml (2 tbs) each soy sauce and rice or cider vinegar
10 ml (1 dsp) sugar
50 g (2 oz) roasted peanuts

Cut the chicken breasts across the grain into 1 cm (½ in) strips and then across again into 1 cm (½ in) cubes. Mix 5 ml (1 tsp) cornflour and the egg white with a fork, beating gently not to make it stiff but to break the texture down. Fold the chicken into the egg white mixture. Heat the oil in a wok, add the garlic, ginger and chilli peppers and then the chicken pieces, stirring them well to make sure they separate. Cook for 3 minutes until well browned. Add the spring onions and the orange or tangerine juice and cook for a further 2–3 minutes. Mix together the remaining ingredients for the sauce: the soy sauce, vinegar, sugar, remaining 10 ml (2 tsp) cornflour, and add half a cup of water. Add the mixture to the chicken and stir over a high heat until the sauce goes smooth and glossy. Add the peanuts and stir again. Serve hot.

CHICKEN YAKITORI

This is a Japanese form of chicken kebabs and it's quite a recent introduction to Japan. Although the style of cooking is believed to have been introduced by the Portuguese in the seventeenth century, the Japanese hadn't started eating meat of any sort until about a hundred years ago – they've now taken to it in a big way. In the amazing food hall of a suburban department store in Tokyo I saw an entire section devoted to making and selling various kinds of yakitori, some designed to be taken home and eaten as a convenience food and others hot and ready to be eaten on the spot. My recipe gives a very basic form but the Japanese have developed it to an art where they mix different kinds of chicken meat – thigh, breast, liver – to produce a variety of textures and tastes. The right skewers for this are the bamboo kind you can find in all Chinese grocery stores and a lot of supermarkets. The dunking method I suggest for flavouring the kebabs is surprisingly effective and not at all messy.

90 ml (6 tbs) shoyu sauce (see Ingredients, page 6)
15 ml (1 tbs) sugar

60 ml (4 tbs) white grape juice or Mirin (see Ingredients, page 6)
350 g (12 oz) chicken breast

Put all the ingredients except the chicken into a saucepan together, bring to the boil and simmer for 10 minutes, allowing the volume to reduce by about a third. Allow to cool a little and pour into the tallest, thinnest glass you have. Cut the chicken across the grain into pieces the size of a large postage stamp and about 5 mm (¼ in) thick. Thread these onto skewers, pushing the skewer through both ends of each piece so that it folds up into a sort of V. As you finish each skewer, dip it into the glass of sauce so that the chicken pieces are coated. Put aside. Heat the grill to maximum temperature for 5 minutes. Dip each skewer again before placing on the rack and grill for 3 minutes; dip again and place, other side up, to grill for another 3 minutes; dip again finally and serve. The repeated dipping glazes the chicken pieces so they have a shiny brown and savoury appearance. This dish is best accompanied by one or two other Japanese dishes, followed by rice and tea and some miso soup if you are being strictly traditional (see page 17).

EMPANADAS

One of the most famous dishes of all from Argentina, this is a delicious combination of meat and fruit in a little crisp pie. In the original form the pastry is made at home but I strongly recommend you buy the widely available and very excellent puff pastry. The dish is quite fiddly in its own right. It is however very much worth doing as the pies are unexpected and quite delicious.

450 g (1 lb) puff pastry, the supermarket kind is fine
225 g (8 oz) cooked and chopped chicken
15 ml (1 tbs) oil
1 small onion
half a leek, washed
half a pear
half a peach
15 ml (1 level tbs) plain flour

125 g (5 fl oz) chicken stock
5 ml (1 tsp) paprika
1.5 ml (¼ tsp) ground cumin
1.5 ml (¼ tsp) freshly ground black pepper or ground chilli
15 ml (1 tbs) fresh chopped parsley
salt to taste
oil for deep frying (optional)

To make the filling, peel and finely chop the onion, and trim and finely chop the leek. Heat the oil in a large pan and gently fry the onion and leek until the onion is translucent. Add the flour, stirring it round until it browns, then add the chicken stock, paprika, cumin, pepper or chilli powder and the parsley. Cook for a minute, stirring so it all blends together. Peel and core the pear and remove the stone from the peach. Chop both and add to the chicken. Add both to the sauce and season to taste. Let it cool before making the empanadas. Roll out the pastry until you have a sheet about ⅛ in thick. You then cut it into circles. The size really depends on how big you want the empanadas to be, but tea plate size, about 5–6 inches across is probably about right. Place a generous amount of the filling in the middle of each circle, then fold over and press the sides together so you have what looks remarkably like a Cornish pasty. Crimp the edges together securely so the filling doesn't seep out while you are cooking them. You can either deep fry empanadas or bake them in the oven, which obviously uses a lot less fat. To deep fry them, use a large deep pan and fill it with enough oil so the empanadas float while they are cooking. To test when the oil is hot enough, drop in a small piece of bread, if it sizzles the oil is ready. Don't overcrowd the pan and watch them all the time, turning them so they turn golden evenly on both sides. Drain well on a wire rack.
If you prefer to cook them in the oven, put them on a baking tray, allowing space for them to expand, brush with a little beaten egg and cook in a medium oven, 350°F/180°C/160°C Fan/Gas 4/bottom of an Aga roasting oven, for 25–30 minutes until golden. Serve hot as a starter or as a main course with a green salad.

Empanadas (top); Nigerian River Province chicken soup (bottom)

TRINIDAD CHICKEN

As with so many parts of the Caribbean, Trinidad has a wonderfully mixed culinary background with African, Indian, French, Spanish and English influences. This is a mild coconut-flavoured chicken sauté that's typical of the chicken dishes cooked on the island. It's often eaten not with rice but with roti, a kind of Indian bread very similar to a paratha, but naans that are available on most supermarket shelves these days will do very well as an alternative.

4 chicken portions
5 ml (1 tsp) allspice
1 small chilli
10 ml (1 dsp) lemon grass purée (from a jar)

juice of 1 lemon
90 ml (6 tbs) coconut milk
225 g (8 oz) finely chopped tomatoes

Cook the chicken gently, skin side down, in its own fat until it's brown. Add the allspice, the seeded and finely chopped chilli and the lemon grass purée. Stir until they coat the chicken, add the coconut milk and the same quantity of water, season generously and cook covered for 15 minutes. Add the tomato and the juice of the lemon, stir to make sure the sauce is thoroughly mixed, bring to the boil and cook vigorously for 3–4 minutes before serving.

BAJAN FRIED CHICKEN

This is simply the best fried chicken recipe I've ever had anywhere in the world. They cook it either very well or very badly in Barbados, but I was lucky enough to stay in a great house up in the hills where there was a wonderful cook who showed me the secret of perfect Bajan chicken.

1 medium chicken
1 medium onion, peeled and roughly chopped
1 clove of garlic, peeled
7 ml (1 heaped tsp) ground thyme
1 chilli

2.5 ml (¹/₂ tsp) allspice
1 egg, lightly beaten
30–45 ml (2–3 tbs) flour
5 ml (1 tsp) each salt and pepper
oil for shallow deep frying, enough to give about ¹/₂ in of oil in the bottom of a large pan

Cut the chicken into joints but keep the skin on each piece. Take the onion, garlic, thyme and allspice, chilli and salt and pepper and whizz them together in a food processor until they have formed a smooth paste. Loosen the skin on each piece of chicken and shove the paste in between the flesh and the skin, so the chicken looks a bit mottled. Leave it for at least 1 hour or up to 12 hours in the fridge for the flavours to penetrate. Then roll the chicken pieces in the flour, dip in the beaten egg, roll the pieces in the flour once more so you have a double layer of flour. Fry in half an inch of oil in a big frying pan into which all the pieces will fit. Brown the pieces on both sides and then put the lid on and cook over a moderate heat for about 20 minutes. The chicken will be golden brown, the flavours of the onions and herbs get driven right into the meat and it is just scrumptious! Serve it with baked sweet potatoes with a little butter and salt and pepper, and a nice salad on the side.

KABULI PILAU

Pilaus and polos are eaten across those parts of the world where Arab and Muslim influence has reigned, from the Spanish paella in the West to the pilaus of Bengal. High in the mountains of Central Asia however the town of Kabul has an enviable reputation for its cooking, or did until its recent catastrophes. The great secret ingredient of much Kabuli cooking is, surprisingly, carrots, which in this version of pilau add a marvellous sweetness as well as colour.

1 chicken, cut up, or 8 chicken pieces
(chicken thighs make an excellent
ingredient in this recipe)
30 ml (2 tbs) oil
30 ml (2 tbs) butter
225 g (8 oz) onion

225 g (8 oz) carrot
50 g (2 oz) raisins
5 ml (1 tsp) each coriander, cumin and
black pepper
350 g (12 oz) long grain or basmati rice

In a large pan which will take all the ingredients easily, melt the butter in the oil. Fry the chicken gently until golden on all sides for about 10 minutes. Add the spices and season generously with salt. Cook for another 2–3 minutes. Peel and finely chop the onion and add that. Peel the carrots, cut them into 2.5 cm (1 in) lengths and cut each length into quarters lengthwise. Add those to the onion and stir gently with the chicken and other ingredients. Rinse the rice thoroughly in a colander until the water runs clear. Add enough water to the pan of chicken to cover the meat completely and simmer gently for 10 minutes. Measure the rice in a jug or measuring cup, drain the liquid from the chicken mixture and measure it in the same jug or bowl, adding enough water to provide twice the volume of liquid to rice. Put the rice into the chicken mixture with the liquid and the raisins and simmer for 20–25 minutes over a very low heat. You can put it into a moderate oven, 325°F/160°C/Gas 3/simmering oven of the Aga, if you prefer. Cook until all the liquid has been absorbed by the rice. Serve it gently mixed together on a large plate and garnish with cucumber, raita (page 225) and chutneys.

BRAZILIAN CHICKEN WITH MANGOS

Although it's not much associated with South American cooking, cream is used quite a lot. It's worth remembering that South America is a huge producer of beef, and the obvious by-product, dairy produce, is used in cooking, particularly in the cities. Here it blends the succulence of chicken with the sharp sweetness of mango to make a really light and delicious combination.

2 boneless chicken pieces
1 ripe mango
125 ml (5 fl oz) double cream
15 ml (1 tbs) oil or butter

coriander or parsley
salt and pepper
rice to serve

Cut off the mango 'cheeks'. Peel and cut the flesh into long thin strips. You should get 4–5 from each cheek. Melt the oil or butter in a medium frying pan. Fry the chicken gently for 10 minutes on each side – keeping a lid on it will help. Remove the chicken and turn the mango in the juices until it is warmed through, remove and arrange with the chicken. Pour the cream into the pan and boil for 2 minutes, then pour this carefully over the chicken and mangos and decorate with the coriander or parsley. Serve with a wild and basmati rice mixture for a spectacular presentation.

PEKING DUCK

Perhaps the most famous of all Chinese dishes, Peking Duck is in fact eaten in a comparatively small if important part of that enormous country. It's a style of cooking that demands not the lightweight wok and a charcoal brazier but big ovens and intense heat. The technique of eating Peking Duck is integral to the dish itself. When the duck is roasted its skin, which is by now crisp and separated from the meat, is cut off rather like a kind of crackling – and then the meat is cut off in small pieces and put on a separate plate to be kept warm. The pancakes are steamed to warm them and then spread with hoisin sauce or a sweet and sour plum sauce made for the purpose. They are sprinkled with a little shredded cucumber and spring onion, and a piece of skin and a piece of duck flesh are folded in as a kind of small parcel. When you bite into the parcel you get the combination of the crispy skin, the succulent flesh, the spicy sauce and the crunchy vegetables all at once – it's a really delicious experience. Peking Duck is quite easy to cook and a lot of fun to eat, but it does require a bit of pre-preparation so if you're cooking it for the evening it's best to start in the morning.

1 large oven-ready duck
30 ml (2 tbs) runny honey
15 ml (1 tbs) soy sauce
1 bunch spring onions, trimmed
20 cm (8 in) piece of cucumber, peeled

100 g (4 oz) hoisin sauce (see Ingredients, page 6) or plum sauce
16–20 pancakes (page 179, or bought ones can be used)

At least 6 hours before you're going to roast it, put the duck into a colander and pour over it a kettleful of boiling water, making sure you get some on all sides. This is best done in a sink, very carefully. The purpose is to get the duck skin to shrink rapidly and separate away from the flesh, thus allowing it to go crisp but not greasy when it's roasted. When you've done this, let the duck drain thoroughly and put it somewhere cool (not the fridge) where the skin can dry out. Pre-heat the oven to 210°C, 425°F, Gas mark 7. Put the duck on a rack in a roasting tin so it sits clear of the bottom and roast it for 40 minutes. Meanwhile mix together the honey and soy sauce in a saucepan and heat just enough to amalgamate. Remove the duck from the oven and spread with this mixture. Put the duck back into the oven and turn the heat down to 190°C, 375°F, Gas mark 5 and roast for another 30–40 minutes until the duck is chestnut brown and cooked right through. Take out of the oven and allow to stand for 5 minutes before removing the skin, in small postage-stamp sized pieces, and then as much of the flesh as you reasonably can, onto separate but warmed plates.

Meanwhile, shred the cucumber by grating it lengthwise and chop the spring onions into 2.5 cm (1 in) lengths, then cut these again lengthwise so that they become easily shredded as well. Put the hoisin sauce into 4 shallow saucers, one for each diner, and put the pancakes, wrapped in foil, into the bottom of the oven to warm through 10 minutes before you're ready to eat. To serve, put the plates of duck and duck skin in the middle of the table surrounded by the bowls of shredded cucumber and spring onion, and 2 or 3 piles of warmed pancakes within easy reach of the diners. You'll need a spoon and perhaps a fork to help spread and fill the pancakes but they should be eaten with the fingers.

SPICED QUAILS

This is the dish my father remembered eating after a day's hunting in the forests of his native Bengal. The birds they ate were those they had shot during the day, but you can now buy quails in supermarkets so it's not quite such hard work. Quails are very small birds with a delicate flavour, so the spicing needs to be as light-handed as it can. I think the best way to eat them is half a quail each as a first course eaten with a chapati or paratha, to be followed by other Indian dishes. For special occasions the Raan of Lamb (page 82) would make a stunning follow-up.

60 ml (4 tbs) butter
2.5 ml (½ tsp) each ground cardamom and paprika
1.25 ml (¼ tsp) each ground bay leaves, chilli pepper and cinnamon

4 quails
juice of a lemon

Mash the spices with the butter until thoroughly blended. Spread a layer of this on the breasts and legs of the quails and put a tiny knob inside each bird. Squeeze the juice of a lemon over the quails and place them, packed fairly well together, on a rack in a baking tray. Preheat the oven to 200°C, 400°F, Gas mark 6. Put the quails in to cook for 10 minutes then take them out and baste them with the juices that will have fallen into the pan below the rack. Move them apart a little and put them back to roast for another 10 minutes. Before serving, pour the juices over them again.

MOLE POBLANO

This extraordinary-sounding dish, turkey in a chocolate sauce, is in fact the national dish of Mexico – Mole is the name given to sauces that are eaten with all kinds of meat. They always contain chillies of one sort or another but very rarely do they contain chocolate because, from pre-colonial times (and this dish dates from the Aztecs) chocolate was a royal ingredient. Only the royal family and their immediate court were allowed to taste it, and women, however high their rank, never got any! My recipe is for the classic turkey version of the Mole Poblano but you can make it, varying the quantities accordingly, with chicken. The original recipe also calls for a variety of different kinds of chilli which are scarcely available here. I suggest you use a couple of ripe sweet red peppers and one or two fresh chilli peppers, the long, thin finger-sized chillies, but use them sparingly because the dish is not meant to be highly spiced but, rather, richly flavoured. It's very definitely a party dish and will feed 8 to 10 people depending on their appetites. It's served with rice and guacamole (an avocado purée flavoured with lime juice and oil, with red and green bell peppers, a little onion, and a little finely chopped tomato stirred in). In Mexico they serve tortillas with it as well.

1 small turkey weighing around 3–4 kg (7–8 lb), jointed into serving pieces
60 ml (4 tbs) cooking oil
1 large onion, peeled and roughly chopped
2 cloves garlic, peeled
2 red peppers, trimmed and de-seeded
1 chilli pepper, trimmed and de-seeded
400 g (14 oz) tin Italian-style chopped tomatoes

2 slices white bread, roughly cut
50 g (2 oz) each almonds, peanuts and sesame seeds
2.5 ml (½ tsp) each ground allspice, star anise (see Ingredients, page 6) and ground coriander
50 g (2 oz) plain bitter chocolate
salt and pepper
chopped fresh coriander

Put the turkey pieces to poach in water in a large saucepan for about 45 minutes, or until the turkey begins to be tender. Drain, keeping the stock, and fry the turkey pieces in oil in a large pan into which they will all fit. Take out the turkey when all the pieces have browned and keep the oil in the pan. Put the onions, garlic, peppers, tomatoes and bread into a food processor and blend to a paste. You can do this by hand if you like but it takes a long time and a lot of trouble.
   Put the paste into the frying pan to fry in the oil. Meanwhile put all the nuts, seeds and the spices into the processor (which you don't need to wash) and process until finely chopped. Add the spice mixture to the tomato and pepper mixture and sauté in the oil for about 5 minutes. Add 400 ml (¾ pint) of stock in which the turkey was cooked, and the chocolate, broken into

small pieces. Check for seasoning. Bring the sauce to a gentle boil until the chocolate has melted. Stir thoroughly and add the turkey pieces, simmering them for about 25 minutes. Put into a serving bowl and decorate with a little chopped coriander or parsley and some more sesame seeds toasted in a dry pan. Serve with white rice, guacamole (page 227), and, if you like, some refried beans.

FASANJAN

This exotic casserole of pheasant cooked in pomegranate juice and thickened with walnuts comes from what used to be called Asia Minor. It is eaten in Iran, in parts of Afghanistan and in the areas of Russia that used to be the emirates of Samarkhand and Bokhara. It's not difficult to come by the ingredients in this country, certainly not in the autumn when pheasant, imported pomegranates and fresh walnuts all arrive in the shops at the same time. It's very rich and, I think, extremely delicious.

1 pheasant, cut into serving pieces
30 ml (2 tbs) butter
1 onion, peeled and finely chopped
150 g (6 oz) walnuts, finely ground

3 fresh pomegranates
salt and pepper
juice of a lemon
15 ml (1 tbs) sugar

Fry the pheasant pieces in the butter until brown. Add the chopped onions, then the ground walnuts and stir for 2 minutes. Squeeze the pomegranates, either using an orange squeezer which works surprisingly well, or putting the bright red seeds scooped out of the shell into a liquidizer and then straining the juice. You need to make it up to about 250 ml (½ pint). Add this to the pheasant, cover and cook gently on top of the stove for about 35–45 minutes until the meat is tender. Season generously and check for a balance of sweet and sour, using the sugar and lemon juice to get it right. Different pomegranates have different degrees of sweetness in them. The sauce will thicken from the walnuts. It should ideally be eaten with a good rice pilau and a crisp salad to follow.

THAI FLAVOURED TURKEY STIR-FRY

I'm afraid this recipe is a bit of a cheat because, to the best of my knowledge, turkey hasn't yet reached Thailand as a generally useable meat. Also the Thais cook their spices slightly differently from this stir-fry technique which is essentially Chinese. However, Thai spicing and flavouring is so distinctive and goes so well with turkey in this very simple and quick recipe that I include it as a crafty interpretation of their cookery style.

450 g (1 lb) turkey stir-fry pieces (or turkey breasts sliced into 1 cm (½ in) slices)
1 onion, peeled and sliced
1 clove of garlic
10 ml (1 dsp) each lemon grass, ginger and chillies, fresh crushed
1 tin coconut cream

1 lime
100 g (4 oz) button mushrooms
50 ml (2 fl oz) sunflower or peanut oil
seasoning

Heat the oil in a wok or large frying pan. Stir-fry the turkey pieces until they are lightly golden, about 5 minutes. Add the onion and the chopped garlic and stir-fry for another minute. Add the coconut cream, the lemon grass, ginger and chillis. Season and simmer for 10 minutes until the spices float to the top of the mixture in a pale red film. Don't worry – this just means that they've cooked through. Wash and halve the button mushrooms and add those with the juice of the lime. Simmer for 1 minute over a high heat and serve with boiled rice and a salad.

MEAT

Of all the many glories of British cooking, the only one that has gained an irreplaceable role in people's hearts is roast beef and Yorkshire pudding, usually served with two veg. The Sunday roast is one of the few remaining indigenous dishes in a country whose cooking has been greatly influenced by foreign cuisines. But the British way of treating meat is about as far removed as you can get from most exotic ways of handling it.

Considering how few kinds of meat people eat on any scale, the range of dishes, methods of cooking and treatment, is just colossal. From just one part of the Indian sub-continent, for example, come recipes for a whole leg of lamb marinated for days in spices and yoghurt, and for minced lamb cooked for just twenty minutes before it's served. Minced lamb, baked with only slightly differing spices, produces a totally different dish 3,000 miles away across the Indian Ocean in the Cape Malay communities in South Africa.

I've got a splendid selection of exotic meat dishes here, principally based on lamb and beef with one or two unusual additions. Some of these dishes, like Jamaican Stew Peas, are meals in themselves and others are meant to be eaten as part of a larger meal. Let me particularly recommend a couple of dishes that may at first sight seem unlikely. The Korean version of Steak Tartare, served with pears and sesame seeds, is truly delicious and the West African Groundnut Stew, although much derided in some colonial memoires, is a tasty and very nutritious way of cooking stewing beef. I've also included one or two dishes of offal, partly because, in most parts of the world where meat is much harder to come by than it is in Britain, very few things are thrown away. In the Middle East I've even been offered baked spleen and vinegared spinal column in my time. You will be relieved to know that neither of those are in this book, but I think you might enjoy Chilli-Fried Liver. In fact I think you'll enjoy all of these crafty exotic meat dishes.

Raan of lamb, peas pilaf, lemon sag, coconut chutney, aloo gobi, spiced quails

RAAN OF LAMB

This is one of the grandest dishes of all Indian cooking. It comes from the north of India and it requires a little time but not very much hard work. It's meant to be served at a special occasion and, when it's cooked, will be so tender that carving will be unnecessary – you can serve it with a spoon and fork. To go with it I suggest Peas Pilau (page 167), Lemon Sag (pages 144–5) and Aloo Gobi (page 144). Chutneys, poppadums and some raita (page 225) all help to make up an Indian feast.

1 leg of lamb weighing 2–2.5 kg (5–6 lb)
5 cm (2 in) piece fresh root ginger, peeled and roughly chopped
10 cloves garlic, peeled and roughly chopped
1 lemon, cut into 8 pieces, pips removed
5 ml (1 tsp) ground cardamom
5 ml (1 tsp) cumin seeds
5 ml (1 tsp) turmeric

5 ml (1 tsp) chilli powder
10 ml (2 tsp) ground coriander
2.5 ml (½ tsp) ground cloves
10 ml (1 dsp) salt
125 g (5 oz) ground almonds
60 ml (4 tbs) brown sugar
500 ml (1 pint) plain yoghurt
1.25 ml (¼ tsp) ground saffron

Trim as much fat as possible off the leg of lamb. Put the garlic, ginger, lemon, cumin, cardamom, cloves, turmeric, chilli powder, coriander and salt all into a food processor or liquidizer and process together until they form a paste. Place the leg of lamb in a baking tray or on a large plate that will go in the fridge. Spread the lemon and garlic paste over it and then put into the same food processor, which you don't have to wash, the almonds, half the brown sugar, the yoghurt and saffron. Blend them together and spread that mixture, in turn, over the lamb, covering it all completely. Put it in the fridge and leave it to marinate for at least 2 and not more than 3½ days. With the lamb in a baking tin, sprinkle the remaining sugar over the top, then put it into a preheated very hot oven (210°C, 425°F, Gas mark 7) and bake it for an hour. Turn the oven down to 160°C, 315°F, Gas mark 2, cover the lamb with a piece of foil, without wrapping it tightly, and bake for another 2 hours. Switch the oven off and allow it to rest for another hour.
To serve, lift the lamb out of the tin very carefully and pour all the juices into a saucepan. Give these a quick boil to reduce and mix them, and serve the lamb in generous portions with the sauce poured over it.

BOBOTIE

Although its roots are in South Africa's Cape Town, where the Cape Malay people were brought to work in the nineteenth century, Bobotie is remarkably similar in its ingredients to the Keema curry above. A different treatment, however, produces a very different result. This is without doubt one of the most popular dishes I know. As soon as anyone comes across it, they become addicted and as it's very easy to make and very economical this is a great blessing. It's traditionally served with yellow rice (long grain rice cooked with turmeric, raisins and sometimes a little coconut milk), and with a set of relishes traditional in Cape Malay cooking which include raw grated carrot salad, grated coconut, chutneys, sliced cucumber in a little vinegar, chopped peanuts, and many others. I like it served with yellow or white rice and a good crisp salad.

250 ml (½ pint) milk
2 slices bread
2 onions, peeled and finely chopped
1 clove garlic, peeled and finely chopped
cooking oil
15 ml (1 tbs) mild curry powder or your own mix (see Ingredients, page 5)

freshly ground black pepper
450 g (1 lb) minced lamb (or beef)
60 ml (4 tbs) chutney or apricot jam
25 g (1 oz) slivered almonds
5 ml (1 tsp) salt
2 eggs

Pour half the milk onto the bread and allow it to soak. Fry the onion and garlic gently in a little oil until translucent. Mash the bread either with a fork or your hands and add to it the onion and garlic mixture, the spices, the meat, the chutney or jam, half the slivered almonds, and the salt. Mix together thoroughly – the easiest way to do this is with your hands. Pack the mixture into a baking dish or gratin dish to a depth of about 4 cm (1½ in). Beat the eggs with the remaining milk and pour this over the top, then add the remaining slivered almonds. Decorate with lemon slices or bay leaves arranged in a little group in the middle. Bake in a preheated medium oven (180°C, 350°F, Gas mark 4) for 45–50 minutes until the meat is cooked through and the custard on the top has set and turned golden. You may need to cover the top for the last 10 or 15 minutes with a piece of foil to prevent the custard burning before the meat has finished cooking. Serve hot in slices like a pie.

MOROCCAN KEBABS

These kebabs from the other end of Africa are known as Quotban and are another example of how differently similar ingredients can turn out when cooked with subtle variations. This is a dish that pays little attention to modern concerns over animal fat consumption, as the cubes of lamb are interspersed with small cubes of beef fat which are cooked on the skewer to provide a total contrast in texture and taste to the lamb itself. I think the old method of alternating a cube of lamb with a cube of suet is really too damaging to health, so I suggest that on each skewer you put one or perhaps two cubes of beef suet to break up the lamb. The meat can be served on the skewers or it can be removed and piled into a small nest of rice for each diner before serving. I think the meat benefits from a generous piece of lemon on the side to squeeze over it.

1 kg (2 lb) boned lamb, with fat removed
3 cloves garlic, peeled
2.5 ml (½ tsp) salt
2.5 ml (½ tsp) each ground cinnamon,
chilli powder, cardamom seeds, freshly
ground black pepper

10 ml (1 dsp) ground ginger
30 ml (2 tbs) each olive oil and lemon juice
225 g (8 oz) beef suet cut into 2 cm (¾ in)
cubes
chopped parsley to serve

Cut the lamb into walnut-sized pieces. Crush the cloves of garlic with the salt and mix them and all the other spices together with the lemon juice and olive oil. Marinate the lamb in this mixture for at least 2 and up to 12 hours. Thread the lamb onto skewers, 4 or 8 cubes to each, depending on how big your skewers are, with one of two cubes of the beef suet interspersed amongst them. Put some foil in your grill pan to catch any spills. Heat the grill for at least 10 minutes before you begin to cook, and grill the kebabs for 3 or 4 minutes on all 4 sides. They are eaten very well cooked and you need to grill them until the beef fat has crisped on the outside and the lamb is thoroughly brown. Sprinkle with chopped parsley when you serve.

Moroccan kebabs

Cous Cous with harissa sauce, Tunisian carrot salad

MUTTON COUS COUS

Mutton is surprisingly hard to find in Britain these days. We used to regard it as a great treat, more so than lamb which was thought to be rather insipid in flavour. Our preferences are now for the tenderness of lamb over the flavour of mutton, but if you can find mutton, it makes a surprising difference to this dish. If you can't, buy the maturer New Zealand lamb.

225 g (8 oz) each carrots, green beans, onions and courgettes or turnips
2 cloves garlic, peeled and chopped
1 kg (2 lb) mutton or lamb, cut into 8 pieces (bone included)
30 ml (2 tbs) olive oil
225 g (8 oz) chick peas (soaked for 4–6 hours and boiled for 1½ hours)

5 ml (1 tsp) each ground ginger and ground cinnamon
5 ml (1 tsp) salt
2.5 ml (½ tsp) saffron powder (optional)
450 g (1 lb) cous cous
500 ml (1 pint) warm water
50 g (2 oz) butter
50 g (2 oz) fresh parsley, chopped

Trim or peel all the vegetables and cut up into 1 cm (½ in) chunks. Fry the garlic gently with the mutton in the oil. After 5 minutes add all the hard vegetables and the chick peas and cover generously with water. Add the salt, cinnamon, ginger and saffron powder if used, and simmer for 45 minutes to 1 hour until the mutton is tender. Meanwhile, in a basin, mix the cous cous with half the water, working carefully through it with a fork or your fingers to remove any lumps. The grain will absorb all the water very quickly. Pile this into a colander that you can safely place on top of the saucepan in which the meat is cooking, without it touching the stew. Half an hour before the end of the cooking time, place the colander over the stew and cover it till the steam is rising clearly through it. After 15 minutes, remove the colander from the stew and gently stir the remaining warm water into the cous cous which, once again, should absorb it and now become swollen almost to the size of rice grains. Cut the butter into small pieces, place them on top and return the cous cous to the stew to continue steaming. Add the softer vegetables (beans and/or courgettes) and cook for another 15 minutes.
To serve, pile the cous cous on to a large serving-plate and hollow it out in the centre. With a slotted spoon remove the vegetables and meat and pile them in the middle. Sprinkle the chopped parsley over the meat and vegetables and serve the liquid in a separate jug. Serve with a spicy Harissa Sauce (page 117). Beware – it is formidable!

PENANG-STYLE LAMB

The Island of Penang in the northern part of Malaysia has a wonderfully cosmopolitan cuisine influenced by the Indonesians, the Malays themselves, and the Chinese. As in the not too distant island of Singapore, this mixture has produced a cuisine where few of the old rules matter any longer, and a dish is judged by its flavour, texture and spiciness. This is an Indonesian-influenced dish with a sauce reminiscent of that used on some of the saté kebabs that are also popular all over South East Asia. There are no skewers involved in this, though, and the dish is extremely succulent and delicious. It should be eaten with rice and one of the South East Asian salads like Gado Gado (pages 157–8), together with a soup. This will make a balanced Malaysian meal.

1 onion, peeled and finely chopped
2 cloves garlic, peeled and finely chopped
2.5 cm (1 in) piece fresh root ginger, peeled and finely chopped
15 ml (1 tbs) oil
700 g (1½ lb) shoulder of lamb, boned
2.5 ml (½ tsp) chilli powder

2.5 ml (½ tsp) ground coriander
60 ml (4 tbs) soy sauce
1½ cups water
60 ml (4 tbs) peanut butter
15 ml (1 tbs) each lime or lemon juice and soft brown sugar

Fry the onion, garlic and ginger in the oil for a minute until the onion begins to turn translucent. Cut the lamb into pieces half the size of a walnut and add them to the ginger and onion mixture. Cook gently for 3 or 4 minutes. Add the spices and the soy sauce plus a cup of water and simmer for 25–30 minutes, until the meat is tender. Stir in the peanut butter and bring gently back to the boil until the sauce thickens and goes glossy and smooth. You may need to add a little more water if it has all dried out in the first cooking. Add the brown sugar and lemon juice and stir gently to mix. Take off the heat and allow to stand for 2 or 3 minutes before serving.

MONGOLIAN HOT POT

This is one of the original communal dishes. In Mongolia it's cooked on a special stove that sits in the centre of the table, with a tall chimney in the middle for the charcoal fumes to escape and a kind of moat around the edge in which the stock sits. These stoves are obtainable in some Chinese stores but a fondue pot or even a saucepan over a night light does just as well.

1 kg (2 lb) lamb fillet or boned leg of lamb
frozen for 2 hours in the freezer
2 bunches spring onions, trimmed and cut
into 5 mm (¼ in) pieces

100 g (4 oz) button mushrooms, trimmed
and cut into 5 mm (¼ in) slices
4 eggs
4 large leaves from a Chinese cabbage

Dipping Sauces

90 ml (6 tbs) soy sauce
60 ml (4 tbs) cider or white wine vinegar
15 ml (1 tbs) sea salt mixed with 15 ml
(1 tbs) ground black pepper

60 ml (4 tbs) oil mixed with 5 ml (1 tsp)
Tabasco or chilli sauce
120 ml (8 tbs) hoisin sauce (see Ingredients,
page 6)

Slicing across the grain, cut the lamb into wafer-thin slices. Then prepare the dipping sauces. Pour the soy sauce and vinegar into separate small bowls, one for each diner (egg cups are fine for this). Heat the salt and pepper together in a non-stick pan for 5 minutes until the pepper releases its aroma. Cool and put on 4 saucers. Put the chilli oil and hoisin into small bowls. Provide each diner with a bowl of rice, a pair of chopsticks, a Chinese or ordinary soup spoon and an empty bowl.

Bring 1 litre (2 pints) of water to the boil and arrange the lamb slices in neat patterns on plates for each diner. Place the saucepan or Mongolian hot pot with the water in it in the middle of the table. Each diner picks up a piece of meat with the chopsticks, dips it in the water for about 30 seconds until it is cooked through, mixes a selection of the condiments and sauces in the empty bowl, dips the meat in that, and pops it in his or her mouth. This goes on until all the meat is used up. You then put the chopped onions and the sliced mushrooms into the broth. Break the eggs carefully into the spoon-shaped ends of the Chinese cabbage leaves, and hold in the saucepan to poach. Remove the egg to the bowl, spoon the soup over it and finish the meal with this. You could omit the egg process and simply eat the broth with the onions and mushrooms cooked in it.

LAMB POLO

This is a dish from the part of Asia where many borders meet. Iran, the Soviet Union and Afghanistan all have traditions of this sort of cooking. The polo is a relation of the Indian pilau and the Spanish paella and they all share the same root name; however this dish is enlivened by the interesting mixture of fruits and nuts that goes in with the meat. Lamb Polo has been a favourite of mine ever since I first tasted this mixture of meat and fruit in Iran many years ago. I was staying near one of the big universities, and eating at the restaurant there was an amazing experience – huge, rather battered-looking aluminium trays would appear, full of the most exquisite food, to be followed, under the light of the stars, by spiced tea which was sipped while listening to gentle and intricate songs sung by some of the nomads from the area. This dish is always served as a *koresh*, that is, a stew to be eaten with the Persian-style rice for which you will find the recipe on page 163. A green salad is usually served with it.

700 g (1½ lb) boned shoulder of lamb or mutton	*1 onion, peeled and finely chopped*
100 g (4 oz) dried apricots	*50 g (2 oz) butter*
100 g (4 oz) dried pears (the white kind are nicest)	*2.5 ml (½ tsp) ground cinnamon*
juice of half a lemon	*2.5 ml (½ tsp) each ground cloves and black pepper*
	salt

Cut the meat into pieces half the size of a walnut. Soak the dried fruit in enough water to cover, with the juice of the lemon added. Bring the fruit to the boil and simmer for 10 minutes. Fry the onion and the meat in the butter, then add the spices and the fruit mixture with its liquid. There should be just enough juice to cover the lamb; if not, add a little more water until it just reaches the top. Simmer for 35–40 minutes and season generously with salt. The meat and fruit should be cooked through and the fruit should have partially disintegrated to thicken the sauce.

Persian grilled lamb

PERSIAN GRILLED LAMB

Another favourite dish from my travels in Iran is this version of grilled lamb. It's not the grilling that's so important but the way that it's served. It seems at first to be a slightly extraordinary set of ingredients and practices, but it produces one of the most delicious dishes I know. I had it every day for lunch for a week and never tired of it.

4 lamb neck fillets, each weighing 150 g
(6 oz)
juice of 2 lemons
60 ml (4 tbs) olive oil

2 large Mediterranean-style tomatoes, cut
in half horizontally
4 egg yolks
100 g (4 oz) butter
450 g (1 lb) long grain rice, cooked
10 ml (2 tsp) sumac (optional)

Cut each fillet of lamb lengthways into two. Squeeze the lemon juice over the lamb, then spread with half the olive oil and leave to marinate for up to 1 hour. Score the tomatoes with a knife and spread with the remaining olive oil. Heat your grill to maximum heat for 10 minutes. Put on the rack the lamb pieces and the tomatoes, cut side up. Grill for 5 minutes per side for the lamb and 10 minutes for the tomatoes.

To serve, each diner should have a plate with a generous portion of hot Persian-style rice. Give each diner an egg yolk, 25 g (1 oz) butter, half a tomato and 2 strips of lamb on a separate plate. The sumac, if used, should be available in the middle of the table. Each diner mixes the egg yolk with the rice and butter, breaks up the tomato with a fork and spreads it on the top of the rice, and then puts the lamb on top of that, flavouring it with the sumac if wished. You cut the lamb up into pieces and eat it, with the rice, already enriched with the egg yolk and butter, absorbing the juices from the meat and the tomato. The taste and flavour combinations are just exquisite.

BEEF STEW WITH FRUIT

This casserole is typical of a range of meat and fruit mixtures that are to be found throughout the cuisine of South America, from Mexico down to Argentina. There is a theory that the Spanish brought the combination with them when they invaded South America, that they in turn got it from the Moors they threw out of Spain in the fifteenth century, who had had it from the Middle East, where combinations of lamb and fruit have long been popular. It seems a far-fetched connection but many of the main ingredients that we take for granted in our cooking, from potatoes and tomatoes to chocolate, have all made the reverse journey from South America to us in a great deal less time, so maybe the idea is true after all. The casserole can be made from a variety of fruits, depending on season and availability. Peaches, apples and pears are perhaps the easiest to buy at the same time in this country, but supermarket shelves these days are full of exotic fruits, such as guavas and paw paws, melons and grapes, so use a combination of not less than two and not more than three fruits. Although it's often served with rice, this is also eaten in many parts of South America with potato cakes, made with a little chopped onion and fried in butter.

1 kg (2 lb) stewing beef, cut into walnut-sized pieces
45 ml (3 tbs) oil
1 onion, peeled and chopped
250 ml (½ pint) water or beef stock
2 apples, 2 pears and 1 peach, peeled, cored or stoned, and chopped (or substitute similar fruits in the same quantities)

225 g (8 oz) tinned Italian tomatoes
5 ml (1 tsp) sugar
150 ml (5 fl oz) double cream or natural yoghurt
salt and pepper

Fry the meat in the oil until brown. Added the chopped onion, cover with the stock or water and simmer until tender. This will depend on the cut of beef but will probably take about 1½ hours. In a separate pan, put the chopped fruit with a ladleful of water or stock, the tomatoes and the sugar. Simmer until the fruit is soft, then either purée in a blender or food processor or push through a sieve. Add the cream, which is usually used, or the yoghurt, which I prefer for a slightly sharper taste. Take the meat out of the stock in which it was cooked, check for seasoning, and pour the specially made sauce over it. The stock makes a lovely basis for soup or pilau for another dish.

Beef stew with fruit, potato cakes

Steak with salsa criolla, lime cordial

STEAK WITH SALSA CRIOLLA

Many countries claim to have the most tender beef but Argentinian 'baby beef', meat that's too old to be veal but too young to be in any way tough, has one of the best claims. For high days and holidays it's cooked at an *Asado Criollo* or Creole Roast; barbecues over great pits full of charcoal with tender cuts of meat grilling over them. One surprising thing about these barbecues is that the meat is never basted with anything except salt and water mixed together into a brine, which not only seasons the meat but seems to form a shiny glazed coating on the outside as well. Once the meat is cooked, it is eaten with various sauces, together with bread and a variety of salads. Depending on which area you're in and the taste of your host, the Criolla sauce can be mild or murderous. I've given the recipes for small quantities of a mild one to be eaten with steaks that are either grilled over a barbecue or cooked under a really hot grill in your own kitchen.

100 g (4 oz) ripe tomatoes, cut in half
1 red and 1 green pepper, de-seeded and cut into chunks
1 bunch spring onions, trimmed and chopped
1 cup each olive or salad oil and wine or cider vinegar

7.5 ml (¹/₂ tbs) each paprika and dry English mustard
2.5 ml (¹/₂ tsp) cayenne pepper
4 sirloin or rump steaks, each weighing about 225 g (8 oz)
15 ml (1 tbs) salt
1 cup warm water

Put all the vegetables into a liquidizer or blender (they can be finely chopped by hand but it's really tedious). Add the liquids, spices and a little salt and process until fairly thoroughly chopped but not a smooth purée. People help themselves to this sauce, from a bowl in the middle of the table, with the grilled steaks. For rare steaks, grill 3 minutes a side under a really hot grill; for medium, 4¹/₂–5 minutes a side; and for ruined, 6–7 minutes. Baste with the 15 ml (1 tbs) salt dissolved in the cup of water, as they cook.

BEEF TERRIAKI

The subtlety of Japanese cooking is in total contrast to the spice and fire of South American cooking. This is a very simple dish loved by Japanese and foreigners equally. You can serve it western style, with potatoes and a salad, or Japanese style with rice and quick stir-fried vegetables and perhaps a bowl of soup to precede it. Sometimes, instead of whole steaks, the Japanese cook tiny slices of beef, about the size of two hazelnuts, in this manner and when they are ready they are placed in a bowl over a minute brazier. This is how Beef Terriaki was cooked for me in a memorable meal eaten in a great, bare bamboo-lined room one autumn evening in Kyoto, the ancient capital of Japan. Sometimes I cook it that way too.

90 ml (6 tbs) shoyu sauce
30 ml (2 tbs) sugar
60 ml (4 tbs) sweet wine grape juice or
Mirin (see Ingredients, page 6)

4 sirloin steaks, each weighing about 150 g
(6 oz), lightly beaten
15 ml (1 tbs) oil

Put all the ingredients except the steak and oil into a saucepan. Bring to the boil and simmer for 5 minutes. Allow to cool and marinate the steaks in the mixture for at least half an hour. Remove and drain. Heat the oil in a big frying pan or steak pan in which the steaks will all fit at one time and cook for 2 minutes on one side and 1 minute on the other. Then add the marinating sauce and boil vigorously until it's reduced to a shiny glaze. Turn the steaks for 1 minute in the sauce and then remove, while the sauce finishes reducing. Pour the remaining sauce, which should not be more than a cupful, over the steaks and serve hot.

GROUNDNUT STEW

The proper name for this in the local pidjin is Ground Nut Chop, an interesting example of how the colonial influences of Britain stretched from China to the west coast of Africa. This is a dish that is often derided in novels about colonial and post-colonial life but in fact it's a delicious and extremely nutritious meal. The ground nuts are of course what we call peanuts and they are used as a crunchy and tasty topping to a rich, spicy stew. This is eaten either with rice or with *egusi*, a kind of grain-like food made from the seeds of the African bitter melon. In many parts of West Africa *egusi* is the staple food: it is obtainable, both as whole seeds and in the ground form, in some places in this country, particularly in shops specializing in Ghanaian and Nigerian products.

30 ml (2 tbs) oil (peanut or soya)
1 onion, peeled and quite finely chopped
1 green pepper (sweet), de-seeded and chopped small
2 small fresh chilli peppers, de-seeded and chopped small
700 g (1½ lb) stewing beef (chuck steak is best for this), cut into 1 cm (½ in) cubes

450 g (1 lb) ripe tomatoes, chopped very small
15 ml (1 tbs) tomato purée
1 sprig fresh or 15 ml (1 tsp) dried thyme
2 bay leaves
salt and pepper
150 g (6 oz) raw skinned peanuts

Heat the oil in an ovenproof casserole and fry the onion, pepper and chillis together. Add the meat and stir until brown. Add the tomatoes, tomato purée and herbs and season generously. Cover and simmer, either on top of the stove or in the oven (180°C, 350°F, Gas mark 4) for 1–1¼ hours till the stew is cooked. In a separate pan, dry-fry the peanuts over a medium heat until they're golden, shaking the pan regularly – this should take about 3–4 minutes. Put them into a food processor or liquidizer and grind them so that they still maintain much of their shape. Spread the nuts over the stew and put back in the oven or on top of the stove for 10 minutes before serving.

BEEF AND SNOW PEAS NOODLE STIR FRY

Stir fries and stir-fried noodles are one of the great basic dishes of Chinese cookery. I think beef lends itself particularly well to this kind of cookery because, unlike some meats, it's actually at its nicest slightly underdone, but with the outside seared. Combining it, as in this recipe, with a really crisp vegetable like mangetout or snow peas produces a marvellous texture contrast as well. One of the great tricks in Chinese stir fry cookery is to cut all the ingredients into a similar size. This serves two purposes: it helps to cook things evenly and in the same time but, furthermore, it's an aesthetic conceit to have all the ingredients the same shape. If you're using noodles this can often mean cutting the ingredients into thin, flat lengths. Both snow peas and sirloin steak are ideal for this.

225 g (8 oz) broad flat noodles (tagliatelle will do, but the Chinese make one about twice as wide, which is ideal)
225 g (8 oz) sirloin steak
30 ml (2 tbs) cooking oil
1 clove garlic, peeled and finely chopped

1 cm (½ in) piece fresh root ginger, peeled and finely chopped
225 g (8 oz) mangetout peas
50 g (2 oz) soy sauce
5 ml (1 tsp) sugar

Bring the saucepan of water to the boil, put in the noodles, cook for 3 minutes, then switch off and cover, leaving aside. Trim any fat and gristle off the steak and slice across the steak into narrow ribbon pieces, not more than 5 mm (¼ in) thick. Heat the oil in a wok or a large frying pan. Put in the onion and ginger and allow to heat for not more than 30 seconds. Add the beef and turn rapidly until both sides of all the pieces are lightly browned. Add the peas and stir together for 1 minute. Mix the sugar and the soy sauce together and add them, tossing over maximum heat for another minute until the meat and vegetables are glossy and heated right through. Drain the noodles, pile into a dish, and pour the beef and peas mixture into the centre to serve.

SUKIYAKI

In the town of Kobi in Japan they've developed the rearing of beef cattle to an extraordinary art. Not only are the cattle fed, watered and generally cared for, as you would expect farmers to do, they are also massaged every day in order to make the beef as tender as possible when the animal is slaughtered and eaten. One of the dishes made with Kobi beef is Sukiyaki, literally, beef on a hoe, a Japanese reference to a much more primitive dish which was cooked over an open fire on a broad-bladed hoe as a kind of barbecue grill. In its modern form, however, it's a very sophisticated dish, often used for group entertaining. It's cooked in a pan in the middle of the table, either with the pan placed on an electric or charcoal brazier, or using one of the modern electric frying pans or woks with a heating element. Assemble all the ingredients in advance and they can sit in the fridge for 4 hours or longer, covered carefully in clingfilm. One of the secrets is to make sure that the dish in which all the food is arranged looks as attractive as possible. In Japan they curve the pieces of meat until the centrepiece looks like a flower, a chrysanthemum or a multi-petalled rose, with the greens, browns and whites of the vegetables around them like foliage.

a piece of beef suet 2.5 cm (1 in) square, or
15 ml (1 tbs) oil
90 ml (6 tbs) shoyu sauce
90 ml (6 tbs) water
15 ml (1 tbs) sugar
1 large sweet onion, peeled
1 bunch spring onions, trimmed

225 g (8 oz) fresh spinach leaves, washed
100 g (4 oz) button mushroooms
100 g (4 oz) Udon (wide Japanese) noodles
700 g (1½ lb) fillet steak or sirloin steak
225 g (8 oz) beansprouts
4 eggs

Grease a hot pan with the beef suet or the oil and in a small bowl mix together the shoyu sauce, water and sugar. Slice all the vegetables into 5 mm (¼ in) slices, holding the spinach together in a bundle to make ribbons. Break the noodles into 15–17 cm (6–7 in) lengths and put to soak in hot water for half an hour. Slice the meat into 5 mm (¼ in) slices across the grain, each piece being about 5–7 cm (2–2½ in) long and 2.5 cm (1 in) wide. Put half the meat into the greased pan and cook briskly, stirring with chopsticks, until it is lightly browned on both sides. Add a portion of onion, spring onion and mushroom and half the sauce liquid. Stir and allow to simmer. Into 4 separate bowls, break the eggs and beat them lightly. Put one bowl in front of each diner with a pair of chopsticks. They lift out the meat and vegetables, dip them in the beaten egg, which will form a coating around them from the heat of the food, and eat them directly. You replenish the pan with more meat and a greater variety of vegetables, including beansprouts, finishing with the noodles which are scrambled with any remaining egg from all 4 bowls and eaten as a finale to the meal. Rice and tea and pickles are often served afterwards in formal Japanese meals but I find that eating a little rice *with* it is a good idea.

RENDANG

This dish comes from the Indonesian island of Sumatra. While meat is eaten throughout Indonesia, in Sumatra it tends to be from animals that have been used for other purposes and is often pretty tough. Long, slow cooking is needed to make it really palatable and delicious and Rendang is one of the favourite ways of doing this. It can, in its native home, be fiercely hot and spicy, as most Sumatran cooking can. I've moderated the viciousness of a proper Sumatran recipe, so here is crafty Rendang.

1 large onion, peeled and roughly chopped
2 cloves garlic, peeled and roughly chopped
2.5 cm (1 in) piece fresh root ginger, peeled and roughly chopped
2.5 ml (½ tsp) each ground coriander, turmeric and chilli powder

250 ml (½ pint) coconut milk (see Ingredients, page 5)
450 g (1 lb) stewing beef (chuck steak is probably best for this)
3 stalks lemon grass, crushed
5 ml (1 tsp) salt

Put the onion, garlic, ginger, spices and coconut milk into a blender or food processor and mix to a smoothish paste. Tip this into a thick, preferably non-stick, saucepan and bring to the boil, then simmer for 5 minutes. Cut the meat into long slices 1 cm (½ in) thick and add it, with the crushed lemon grass and salt. Bring to a fast boil and simmer, uncovered, until the liquid has almost all disappeared. Turn the heat right down and simmer until the dish is really dry, allowing the meat to fry gently in the remaining oil and spices until medium brown. Do not let it burn but make sure that the liquid has completely gone. Serve with two or three other Malaysian and Indonesian dishes and possibly a bowl of soup, with plenty of plain boiled rice.

Bobotie (top); Korean beef with pears (bottom)

KOREAN BEEF WITH PEARS

Korean food is very substantial and warming. The country is well to the north and while they have brief hot summers, the winters can be really cold. This dish, surprisingly, isn't cooked – it's a form of steak tartare, but incredibly warming and nourishing nonetheless. Don't be put off by the thought of raw beef: many of us enjoy our roast beef, steak or even hamburgers rare in the middle, after all, and this dish doesn't taste or look uncooked in any way – in fact it's one of my favourites. Like many eastern dishes, it's eaten as part of a large mixed meal with people helping themselves to portions of different dishes. A substantial fried vegetable dish and perhaps a spiced chicken dish would make this a wonderful meal, served with some rice.

30 ml (2 tbs) sesame seeds
4 spring onions, trimmed and finely chopped
450 g (1 lb) lean minced steak
15 ml (1 tbs) sesame oil (see Ingredients, page 6)

60 ml (4 tbs) hoisin sauce (see Ingredients, page 6)
5 ml (1 tsp) salt
2 ripe pears or Japanese-style pears, peeled and cored

Toast the sesame seeds in a smear of oil in a small frying pan until they go golden; set aside. Mix the spring onions, white and green, with the meat, using a fork. Add the sesame oil, salt and the hoisin sauce and mix gently but thoroughly. Mix half the toasted sesame seeds into the meat, pile it into an attractive serving dish, and sprinkle the remaining seeds over it. Slice the pears into quarters, then each quarter into half lengthwise. Arrange these overlapping around the meat as a kind of fence, leaving the centre of the meat uncovered.
To serve, each person takes a couple of slices of pear and the section of meat and sesame seeds underneath them. The combination of the crunchy fresh pear and the richly seasoned meat is delicious.

BHUNA GHOSHT

Roughly translated this name means 'dry meat', and it's a form of curry that can be made with either beef or lamb. This recipe came down to me, through my mother, from a very great Indian lady who used to rule her enormous household in Bombay with a rod of iron. My mother's note to me on the recipe says: 'This can be cooked in the oven, though top of the stove is more traditional. It's meant to be dry when it's finished. The oven takes a little longer but does avoid the danger of burning.' It seems to me to be very good advice.

---

5 ml (1 tsp) each ground coriander and garam masala
1.25 ml (¼ tsp) chilli powder
1 onion, peeled and finely sliced
1 clove garlic, peeled and finely chopped
50 g (2 oz) ghee

450 g (1 lb) beef stewing steak, cut into neat pieces
tamarind water to cover (you could use ordinary water with the juice of a lemon mixed in it)

Mix the spices with some water to make a thick paste. Fry the onion and garlic in the ghee till brown. Add the paste and fry this thoroughly. Add the meat and fry till the juices run. Cover the meat with the tamarind water and simmer for 1½–2 hours till tender and dry. If you are cooking it in the oven, the temperature should be around 170°C, 325°F, Gas mark 3; it helps to uncover the casserole for the last half hour of cooking.

JAMAICAN STEW PEAS

This is one of Jamaica's great dishes and when I lived there I can remember it being served at everything from parties to the staff canteen. The 'peas' of the title are in fact red kidney beans. In Jamaica it can also include one or two rather unusual and slightly difficult to obtain ingredients like salted pig's tail, so this is a crafty version which I think tastes just as good.

450 g (1 lb) red kidney beans
1.5 kg (3 lb) shin of beef, cut into pieces 2.5 cm (1 in) square
1 bunch spring onions, trimmed and crushed
1 chilli pepper, left whole

1 sprig thyme or 5 ml (1 tsp) dried thyme
225 g (8 oz) salt beef or tongue, if available, cut into 2.5 cm (1 in) pieces
1 cup flour
5 ml (1 tsp) salt
2 cloves garlic, peeled and chopped

Soak the kidney beans in water for 3 hours. Put the meat, spring onions and the soaked beans into a pan with the chilli pepper and the thyme. Add the salt beef, if you're using it, and cover generously with water. Bring to the boil and boil for 10–15 minutes, then turn down and simmer, either on top of the stove or in a slow oven (170°C, 325°F, Gas mark 3), until the meat is tender and the beans soft. This can take about 2 hours. If the water starts to dry up, add a little more.

Meanwhile, make dumplings from the flour in the following manner. Sieve the flour and salt together and gradually mix in 1 cup of water, stirring with a fork until it makes a smooth and reasonably soft dough. Pinch pieces about the size of a hazelnut out of the dough and drop into the stew shaped, as they would be from your fingers, into little triangular peaks. An alternative way is to roll the same sized piece of dough between your palms until it forms a long, thin sausage. At the same time add the chopped garlic. Cook the dumplings, of whichever shape, for about 10–15 minutes. They will thicken the stew as well as adding to its texture and flavour. Serve the dish hot with rice, fried plantain (see page 150) and a salad.

PEKING-STYLE DRY SHREDDED BEEF

This is a Chinese dish that is often eaten at the beginning of banquets. It's very different in both taste and texture from the stir fry dishes that we're used to in the west, but it's a marvellous appetizer and/or a contrast to dishes with more plentiful sauces. It can also be cooked very quickly as a snack to be eaten with a little rice that you may have left over in the fridge.

450 g (1 lb) sirloin steak, cut into thin, 5 cm (2 in) long shreds
30 ml (2 tbs) oil
2.5 ml (¹/₂ tsp) each salt and freshly ground black pepper
45 ml (3 tbs) soy sauce
15 ml (1 tbs) chilli sauce (Chinese-style, not Tabasco)

10 ml (2 tsp) sugar
100 g (4 oz) carrot, peeled and cut into matchstick shreds
4 celery sticks, trimmed and cut into matchstick shreds
2.5 cm (1 in) piece fresh root ginger, peeled and shredded

Heat the oil in a wok or thick frying pan, add the beef and cook over a very high heat for 4 minutes. Add the salt and pepper and stir. Pour in the sauces and the sugar and mix. Add the carrot, celery and ginger and toss together for 2–3 minutes until they are heated through and well coated. There should be virtually no liquid left in the dish.

BULGOGI

This is the national dish of Korea, traditionally cooked on the shield that a Korean warrior would take into battle! If this sounds unlikely, it is, like many barbecue dishes, a refinement of a simple practical necessity. It does mean that in Korea and in Korean restaurants the meat is cooked on a device that, rather than being concave like a wok or saucepan, is convex over the heat source. It works particularly well, though a heavy-based frying pan or even a grill or barbecue is fine. Bulgogi tends to be served as a separate course, to be followed by other dishes and rice.

***

4 spring onions, trimmed and finely sliced, keeping the green part
60 ml (4 tbs) soy sauce
30 ml (2 tbs) soft brown sugar
2 cloves garlic, peeled and crushed with a little salt

15 ml (1 tbs) sesame oil
700 g (1½ lb) topside beef, sliced thinly across the grain into strips
15 ml (1 tbs) sesame seeds

Mix the spring onions, the soy sauce, the brown sugar, garlic and the sesame oil. Marinate the beef strips in this soy sauce mixture for 30 minutes to 6 hours. Toast the sesame seeds in a small frying pan until they turn golden. Heat your grill or frying pan (a non-stick one is ideal) until it's very hot. Add the beef, spreading it carefully so that it's in a single layer, and either fry or grill for 2 minutes a side. Sprinkle over the sesame seeds and oil and serve immediately on hot plates.

CHILLI-FRIED LIVER

In Indonesia this dish is cooked with a formidable amount of chilli powder or hot, dried chillies. You can adjust the chilli to your own taste, but don't leave it out altogether or the dish becomes bland.

30 ml (2 tbs) oil
2 small red chillies, de-seeded and finely chopped
5 ml (1 tsp) Laos Powder (see Ingredients, page 6)
1 large onion, peeled and finely chopped
2 cloves garlic, peeled and finely chopped
5 ml (1 tsp) Worcester sauce

1 stalk lemon grass (see Ingredients, page 6)
juice of half a lemon
15 ml (1 tbs) brown sugar
225 g (8 oz) coconut milk (see Ingredients, page 5)
450 g (1 lb) lamb's liver, cut into 2.5 cm (1 in) dice

Heat the oil in a frying pan and add the spices, onion, garlic and Worcester sauce. Fry gently for 5 minutes. Then add the lemon grass, lemon juice, sugar and coconut milk; stir till mixed. Add the liver and cook gently for 15 minutes, until a film of oil appears on the top of the dish.

SOO YOSOPI (Rice Soup)

This wonderfully named dish is almost the national dish of Paraguay, the land-locked country in South America which shares much of its cuisine with its southern neighbours, particularly Argentina. This is a warming soup with a number of unexpected combinations of ingredients which is eaten really as a main course and as a one pot meal rather than as a starter to something more substantial.

450 g (1 lb) lean minced beef
500 ml (1 pint) of water
1 medium onion
15 ml (1 tbs) olive or salad oil
175 g (6 oz) cooked white rice

1 small green pepper
175 g (6 oz) chopped fresh tomatoes
2.5 ml (½ tsp) oregano
15 ml (1 level tbs) chopped fresh parsley
1 tsp salt

Peel and finely chop the onion and trim and de-seed the green pepper and finely chop that as well. Mix the minced beef with the water, blending them thoroughly. Heat the olive oil in a large pan and fry the onion with the pepper and tomato gently until they are all hot through. Add the meat, the cooked rice and the oregano and cook together over a medium heat, stirring constantly, adding a little more water if it starts to dry out. Cook it for about 15 minutes, remove from the heat, add the parsley and salt and serve from soup bowls.

AREPAS

Arepas is the national dish of Venezuela. For reasons best known to the citizens of that country, its name literally means 'old clothes'. I think this is because the meat is shredded once it has been cooked and has a slightly ragged appearance. It could also come from the appearance of the corn meal dumplings it is traditionally served with. It doesn't stop it however being quite delicious. While the dish is usually eaten with the dumplings the flour is almost impossible to get in Britain so I suggest you eat it with the rice and also a dish of black beans cooked with a little chilli and tomato.

700 g (1¹/₂ lb) beef, preferably skirt or good braising steak
2 large onions
1 red and 1 green pepper

15 ml (1 tbs) tomato purée
2.5 ml (¹/₂ tsp) each freeze dried oregano and thyme
salt and pepper

Simmer the beef with the herbs in just enough salted water to cover. The beef should be in big pieces and it should take about 35 minutes, but it could be up to 1 hour depending on the quality of the meat. Remove the meat from the pan and set it aside. Boil the stock until only half a cupful is left. Shred the meat, preferably with forks, into small pieces. Peel, trim and chop the onion and peppers until very small. Place the peppers and onions with the reduced stock and tomato purée into a pan and cook together for 5 minutes. Season generously and return the shredded beef to the pepper mixture. Add the herbs, season, and mix together. Serve with white rice.

KOREAN RICE BOWL

This dish has a wonderful name in Korean: it is 'yukhoioibimbab'. I think, translated, it means beef and vegetables on hot rice, and that's a very good description. It's a one dish meal that has both succulence and freshness. It's also full of the most delicious flavours. It's essential that the rice for this be freshly cooked and absolutely hot.

225 g (8 oz) rice, freshly cooked Chinese
style (see page 166)
100 g (4 oz) each shredded cucumber,
peeled carrot and spinach
100 g (4 oz) beansprouts
30 ml (2 tbs) hoisin sauce

225 g (8 oz) lean coarsely minced beef
4 egg yolks
salt and pepper

Present each diner with a bowl of hot rice and in the centre of the table place a plate with the vegetables arranged separately around it and the meat in the middle. Each diner should also have egg yolk in a small Chinese-style tea cup available to them and a small bowl with some hoisin sauce. To eat the food, you mix a portion of each of the vegetables into the rice with the raw beef and the egg yolk. Season with the hoisin until the whole mixture is thoroughly blended. The heat from the rice will cook the meat and soften the vegetables. It should then be eaten either with chopsticks or, if you prefer it, with a spoon. A bowl of soup, usually clear and similar to chicken noodle, is often drunk as an accompaniment.

LIVER WITH PINEAPPLE

I first had this extraordinary combination for breakfast just off the Venezuelan coast. It seemed unlikely at that time of day but cooked for lunch or dinner has a marvellous sweet and sour combination to it that I think deserves wider recognition. It's meant to be a dry dish so don't be tempted to add any other liquid.

450 g (1 lb) lamb's liver
225 g (½ lb) onions
225 g (½ lb) fresh pineapple, skinned

4 drops chilli sauce
30 ml (2 tbs) oil (not olive)
seasoning

Cut the liver into thin slices, about 5 mm (¼ in) thick, and then cut each slice into approximately 2.5 cm (1 in) squares. Peel the onion and cut that into similar sized pieces, breaking up the rings. Slice the pineapple thinly and cut that into 2.5 cm (1 in) squares as well. Heat the oil in a frying pan and sauté the onion for about 2–3 minutes until it's translucent. Add the liver and cook over a high heat very quickly for just 1 minute. Season, add the chilli sauce and then add the pineapple. Cook for only another minute until the pineapple is hot but not breaking up. Season and serve immediately with rice and some creamy vegetables.

VEGETARIAN DISHES

In Britain and the West we tend to take meat for granted, even though there is a growing and increasingly influential vegetarian movement based on ethical or environmental issues. But in many parts of the world, meat is a comparative rarity. This may be a question of availability, since meat is much more 'expensive' to produce than vegetables and grains, which makes it a luxury in a subsistence or low grade agricultural economy. But in China and much of India there are also religious prohibitions against eating meat. In both Buddhism and Hinduism there is a powerful commitment to a vegetarian diet. Whether from need or choice, the fact is that all over the world there are wonderful cuisines and dishes based on vegetarian principles. Whereas in the West most vegetarian food seems to be an adaptation of meat-based dishes – vegetable lasagne, chilli without the carne, 'nut roast' – the exciting and interesting feature of exotic vegetarian food is that it doesn't make any apologies for not having meat in it.

The dishes in this chapter come from all over the world. From the Far East comes a Tempura from Japan which, until the late nineteenth century, was virtually a meat-free society. More substantially, from South America come recipes devised for their indigenous vegetables, such as potatoes and beans. Some of the recipes are very humble like the Potato-stuffed Parathas, which was taught to me by an aged aunt who made them by hand with great skill and dexterity. Other dishes, like the Cous Cous or the Byriani, are quite elaborate and can be served for special family meals or even smart dinner parties to a rapturous reception. The stir-fried noodles, which were taught me by Kenneth Lo, allows for all kinds of variations in flavour and texture.

Monk's mixed vegetables

MONK'S MIXED VEGETABLES

The name of this dish derives from a legendary recipe served at a Buddhist monastery in the north of China. Nowadays the title is much corrupted and is used to cover anything from a simple vegetable stir fry to a really sophisticated casserole which more closely resembles the original. This is a crafty version which rather splits the difference. Its contents provide a well balanced meal, not only in flavour and texture but also in nutrition. It's the sort of dish on which people who've given up all animal-based products (vegans) can thrive. It has another great virtue for me, which is that it is an example of the more subtle forms of Chinese cooking that the wok and stir frying have tended to make us all forget. It's best eaten as a main course served with a good bowl of rice.

2 blocks tofu (fresh white bean curd)
oil for frying
50 g (2 oz) dried mushrooms (Chinese are
ideal, but Italian will do)
2.5 cm (1 in) piece fresh root ginger, peeled
and finely chopped
1 onion, peeled and finely sliced
a quarter of a Chinese cabbage, sliced into
1 cm (½ in) ribbons

225 g (8 oz) broccoli, cut into small florets
1 small aubergine, halved lengthwise and
cut into 1 cm (½ in) slices
100 g (4 oz) Chinese wheat noodles
30 ml (2 tbs) soy sauce
5 ml (1 tsp) sugar
15 ml (1 tbs) cornflour
salt and pepper
10 ml (2 tsp) sesame oil

Slice each block of bean curd into 4 pieces, to give you 8 pieces roughly the size of a large matchbox. Deep fry these for 3 minutes and put to drain. Put the dried mushrooms to soak in boiling or hot water for 15 minutes. Remove the stalks and cut the mushrooms into 5 mm (¼ in) slices; keep the water. In a deep saucepan, heat 2 tablespoons of oil and fry the ginger with the onion for 3 minutes. Add the rest of the vegetables and stir fry another 4–5 minutes. Add the noodles, the soy sauce, the sugar and the liquid the mushrooms were soaked in. Add enough water to come 1 cm (½ in) above the mixture. Cover and simmer for 15 minutes until the noodles are thoroughly cooked. Mix the cornflour with enough water to make a smooth paste and stir it into the vegetable mixture. Add the fried tofu bean curd, stirring very gently so as not to break it up. Check for seasoning, put the lid back on and simmer another 5 minutes, by which time the sauce should have thickened. Serve it gently into a bowl and sprinkle on the sesame oil to flavour.

VEGETABLE COUS COUS

Cous cous is cracked wheat broken down to grains the size of coarse semolina and then rubbed with very fine flour so it adopts an almost silken texture. It is steamed and then eaten with a variety of sauces and stews all along the Mahgreb, the coastline of North Africa. Styles of sauces, flavourings and presentation vary across Algeria, Tunisia and Morocco, but the central grain, the cous cous itself, is the heart of the cuisine. One of the greatest advantages of modern-day life is that you can get cous cous that has been pre-cooked, so it's now possible to get it ready within 30 minutes instead of the hour and a half's steaming that it used to require. The recipe below is for a traditional seven-vegetable Cous Cous from Algeria. The seven is a 'lucky' number but the individual vegetables can be varied depending upon what is seasonally available. This is very much a family or communal party dish, piled high in the middle of a table on an occasion when many people are eating together. And be warned – it's very moreish. I usually cook enough for two extra guests, whom I'm sure aren't coming. I have included a recipe for a spicy sauce that's traditionally served with Cous Cous called Harissa: it is probably the only onomatopoeic name for a sauce in the whole of cooking, because that's roughly the noise you make when you taste it. Use it sparingly!

450 g (1 lb) cous cous grains
30 ml (2 tbs) olive oil
2 cloves garlic, peeled and chopped
1 large onion, peeled and chopped
225 g (8 oz) carrots, peeled and cut into 1 cm (½ in) chunks
225 g (8 oz) turnips (or swedes), peeled and cut into 1 cm (½ in) chunks
150 g (6 oz) chick peas, soaked and cooked for 2 hours

2.5 ml (½ tsp) each chilli, ground cinnamon and ground ginger
salt and pepper
225 g (8 oz) courgettes, trimmed and cut into 1 cm (½ in) chunks
225 g (8 oz) green beans, trimmed and cut into 2.5 cm (1 in) lengths
15 ml (1 tbs) parsley, chopped
15 ml (1 tbs) butter, cut into small pieces

In a bowl stir 250 ml (½ pint) of cold water into the cous cous with a fork, breaking up any lumps that form; the cous cous will absorb the water almost immediately. Put the olive oil into a saucepan which will take a colander sitting on top of it. Heat the oil and put in the garlic, then the onions, carrots and turnips. Add the drained chick peas, the spices and season generously with salt and some pepper. Cover with water to a depth of 5 cm (2 in) and bring to a gentle boil. Put the cous cous into a colander, adding just a little more water if it's gone very dry. Sit in on top of the stew so that the colander seals the saucepan, without touching the food underneath.

Cover with a lid and allow to steam over the cooking stew for 25 minutes. Take the cous cous colander off the saucepan, add the remaining vegetables and check the cous cous itself. It should have swollen to the size of small grains of rice. Add another cup of warm water and mix thoroughly. Put the butter on top of the cous cous and return the colander to the saucepan for another 5–8 minutes cooking. The courgettes should just be cooked through but not soggy. To serve, remove the cous cous and, stirring it with a fork, pile it up into a large serving dish; hollow it out in the middle. Spoon the vegetables into the gap in the centre of the cous cous, retaining most of the liquid which you can pour into a jug. Serve so that guests can help themselves to cous cous and vegetables and moisten the mixture with the sauce from the jug.

Harissa

1 clove garlic, peeled
2.5 ml (½ tsp) salt
5 ml (1 tsp) chilli sauce (Tabasco type)

2.5 ml (½ tsp) ground cumin
60 ml (4 tbs) cooking liquid

Crush the garlic clove with the salt, mix with the chilli sauce, and dilute with the cooking liquid. The resulting sauce is very powerful and should be used as a seasoning for the vegetables and cous cous.

VEGETABLE BYRIANI

Byrianis are high day and holiday food in the Indian sub-continent. Very often, at special celebrations like weddings or a child's coming of age, a huge outdoor meal is organized with pots of byriani half the height of men being cooked very slowly over carefully tended charcoal fires. A byriani was originally a north Indian dish derived from the same roots as the pilaus, polos, and paellas that stretch from Spain to China. All are rice dishes, usually flavoured with saffron and containing a variety of delicacies. In byrianis the cooking is done in two parts. What we would think of as the 'curry' mixture is cooked, and the rice is parboiled separately. They are then brought together in layers and served (traditionally on a silver tray).

450 g (1 lb) long grain Patna or Basmati rice
30 ml (2 tbs) oil
15 ml (1 tbs) butter
2 cloves garlic, peeled and crushed

225 g (8 oz) carrots, peeled and cut into 1 cm (½ in) chunks
225 g (8 oz) aubergines, trimmed and cut into 1 cm (½ in) chunks
half a cauliflower, broken into florets

2.5 cm (1 in) piece fresh root ginger, peeled and finely chopped
2 large onions, peeled and thinly sliced
5–10 ml (1 heaped tsp) each ground cumin, ground coriander and turmeric
2.5 ml (½ tsp) each chilli powder and paprika (or use 15 ml/1 tbs mild curry powder)
225 g (8 oz) potatoes, peeled and cut into 1 cm (½ in) chunks

100 g (4 oz) stick beans, trimmed and cut into 2.5 cm (1 in) lengths
225 g (8 oz) peas (frozen will do)
5 ml (1 tsp) salt
2.5 ml (½ tsp) crushed saffron or saffron powder
juice of half a lemon
5 ml (1 tsp) soft brown sugar
2.5 ml (½ tsp) garam masala
chopped fresh coriander or parsley to garnish

Rinse the rice in 2 or 3 changes of water and put to soak in plenty of warm water for half an hour. Put the oil and butter into a saucepan and fry the garlic and chopped ginger for 1 minute. Add the onions and fry for another 2 minutes. Add the spices, except the saffron and garam masala, and fry for 2–3 minutes. Add a cup of water, bring to a boil and allow the water to evaporate until the mixture is frying gently again. Add all the vegetables except the peas and enough water to cover. Simmer gently for 10 minutes, adding the peas 5 minutes before the end of the cooking time. Meanwhile, drain the rice, put it in a large saucepan and cover it with water to a depth of 5 cm (2 in) above the rice. Add the salt, bring to the boil and cook for 8 minutes. Drain the rice. In a large casserole, put one third of the rice, then a layer of half the spicy vegetables, leaving most of the liquid behind, another third of the rice, a final layer of vegetables, then the remaining rice to make an even, flat surface. Mix the saffron powder with a little warm water and pour over the rice. Seal the casserole tightly and put into a low oven (170°C, 325°F, Gas mark 3) for 45 minutes to an hour. The rice will continue to cook in its own steam and the flavours of the saffron and spices will intermingle. Meanwhile, if the liquid remaining in the vegetable pan is still considerable, boil it down until it provides about 2–3 cupfuls. Stir in the lemon juice, brown sugar and garam masala. To serve, spoon the rice and vegetable mixture carefully out of the casserole onto a big serving dish, sprinkle it with chopped fresh coriander or parsley and pass the liquid from the vegetables separately as a sauce. The colours and scents are delightful.

VEGETARIAN TEMPURA

This is a vegetarian version of this famous Japanese dish. It can be, and is frequently today, cooked with fish as an addition — prawns that have been shelled, slices of white fish (usually some form of sole) — fried after the vegetables, but I like it as a wholly vegetarian version. There are purists in the cooking of tempura as there are in almost all forms of Japanese cookery, which is a process in which simplicity is intended to be the result of high craftsmanship and skill. In its purest form, tempura is cooked in sesame oil — not the kind of roasted sesame oil that we sometimes use here for flavouring but a very light, pure oil that's used just for frying. I find most good nut or frying oils do extremely well and don't change the taste that much. There are also views about the batter and the batter I've opted for here is the craftiest (and simplest) solution. As with all deep frying, you need to watch the temperature carefully; I find an electronically controlled deep fryer an absolute boon in cooking this sort of food. Give each diner a small bowl for their sauce, so that they may dip in the pieces of crisply fried vegetable before popping them in their mouths.

1 bunch spring onions, trimmed, retaining some green
100 g (4 oz) button mushrooms, washed and trimmed
100 g (4 oz) carrot, peeled and cut into 5 mm (¼ in) rounds

100 g (4 oz) green beans, topped and tailed
1 medium sized sweet potato, peeled and cut into oval rounds 5mm (¼ in) thick
100 g (4 oz) mixed frozen vegetables, defrosted
oil (see above) for deep frying

Batter

1 egg
1 cup plain flour

Sauces

90 ml (6 tbs) shoyu sauce
60 ml (4 tbs) sweet white grape juice or Mirin (see Ingredients, page 6)
½ cup water or dashi (see Ingredients, page 5)

half a Japanese white radish (daikon or mouli), peeled and grated finely
2.5 cm (1 in) piece fresh root ginger, grated finely

Prepare all the vegetables and heat the oil in your deep fryer. Ideally it should be fresh, clean oil, or at least carefully filtered. To make the batter, break the egg into a large breakfast sized cup and add enough cold or iced water to fill the cup. Pour it into a bowl and beat lightly. Measure the flour into the same cup and add that, in one go, to the egg and water. Mix thoroughly but do not worry about lumps. It's important that this is done lightly and not with an electric or mechanical whisk – in Japan they use chopsticks. Without allowing the batter to rest, begin to cook the tempura. Starting with the hard vegetables like sweet potato and carrot, dip them, 5 or 6 pieces at a time, into the batter. Allow any surplus to drain off and slide them gently into the hot oil, which should be at a temperature of 170°C, 350°F if you have a thermostat. Allow to cook for 2–3 minutes, turning, until the batter is crisply gold and the vegetables cooked through. Remove and put onto kitchen paper to drain. Carry on with the other vegetables, finishing with the spring onions. Towards the end of the cooking time you may increase the heat of the oil by 10°C, 20°F as the vegetables are lighter and can be cooked more quickly. Mix the frozen vegetables with the remaining batter and fry spoonfuls at a time in the oil. To make the dipping sauce: mix the shoyu sauce, the grape juice or Mirin, and the water or dashi together and pour a quarter into a bowl in front of each diner. Mix the radish and ginger together and put a spoonful in the middle of each bowl of dipping sauce.

Stir-fried noodles with black bean sauce (top); Aubergine Imam Bayeldi (bottom)

STIR-FRIED NOODLES WITH BLACK BEAN SAUCE

This is an example of the more sophisticated end of Chinese stir fry cookery. We tend to think of stir fry food as everything cooked in the same pan, flavoured with the same sauce, but it can be much more than that. This is effectively a three-level dish which, served on a large oval platter, not only looks attractive but provides a variety of contrasts in taste and texture as any meal should. Served with some kind of soup as a first course and a fruit salad as a last course, it makes a satisfactory meal in its own right, although it can be eaten as part of a larger Chinese repast.

450 g (1 lb) Chinese noodles
60 ml (4 tbs) oil
2.5 cm (1 in) piece fresh root ginger, peeled and finely chopped
2 cloves garlic, peeled and finely chopped
1 bunch spring onions, trimmed and cut into 7.5 cm (3 in) lengths
225 g (8 oz) courgettes, trimmed and cut into long shreds

1 red pepper, halved, de-seeded and cut into thin shreds
225 g (8 oz) beansprouts, washed
30 ml (2 tbs) Chinese black beans or black bean sauce
15 ml (1 tbs) chilli sauce
400 g (14 oz) tinned Italian chopped tomatoes
soy sauce
salt and pepper

Put the noodles to cook in a pan of boiling water with a pinch of salt and a drop of oil. They usually cook more quickly than Italian pasta so don't let them go too far – about 8 minutes is fine. Allow them to rest in the cooking liquid while you make the rest of the dish. In a wok or large frying pan, put 2 tablespoons of the oil and add the ginger, garlic and spring onions. Toss quickly for 1 minute, add the courgettes, red pepper and beansprouts and stir fry for 3 minutes. In a small pan, put the remaining oil, the black beans or black bean sauce, the chilli sauce and the tomatoes. Stir and bring to the boil. Add the soy sauce to the first vegetable mixture and check for seasoning – it may need a pinch of salt. Assemble the dish by draining the noodles thoroughly and stirring one third of the beansprout mixture into them. Put this in a layer in a big oval serving dish or gratin dish. In the centre of that, put the rest of the beansprout vegetable mixture and then, in a third layer in the centre of the vegetable mixture, very carefully pour the tomato and black bean mixture, which should have reduced to the thickness of double cream.

MEXICAN BEAN BAKE

Mexico is the home of many of the beans we eat today, including the kind that we turn into baked beans. Beans are still enormously popular there and are eaten at almost every meal. Apart from the high protein content of almost all beans, they also provide a significant amount of fibre in the diet, so they are an important ingredient for people who have given up or reduced their meat intake. The beans used for this recipe in Mexico and its neighbours in South America are the black beans sometimes called turtle beans. They are available in some health food stores, and if you can find them, don't be put off by their colour – they taste delicious. But otherwise red kidney beans or even white haricot beans cooked in this manner taste good. This dish makes a wonderfully warming casserole for a crisp winter night. Serve it with some tortilla chips, chilli-flavoured crisps that you can buy anywhere in Britain these days. An avocado purée and/or a green salad makes a nice accompaniment.

450 g (1 lb) black or red kidney beans
1 onion, peeled and chopped
1 clove garlic, peeled and finely chopped
2 bay leaves
45 ml (3 tbs) oil (not olive)

2 large tomatoes or 225 g (8 oz) tinned Italian tomatoes, chopped
1 small red or green chilli, seeds removed and finely chopped
5 ml (1 tsp) salt

Soak the beans for at least 4, and preferably 6 hours, in plenty of fresh cold water. Discard the water and put the beans, the onion and garlic, the bay leaves, a tablespoon of the oil, and half the chopped tomatoes into a casserole that will go in the oven. Cover with fresh cold water to a level 2.5 cm (1 in) above the vegetables. Bring the casserole to the boil on top of the stove for 10 minutes, then place it in a medium oven (180°C, 350°F, Gas mark 4) for 1½–2½ hours, depending on the age and size of the beans. When cooked they should be tender but not totally collapsed and almost all the water should have been absorbed. In a separate pan, fry the chopped second tomato and the chilli pepper in the remaining 2 tablespoons of oil and add a ladleful of the beans without their liquid. Mash these up with the tomato and chilli until reasonably smooth and add, with the salt, back to the main casserole. Stir to mix and leave to simmer for another 5 minutes for the flavours to amalgamate and blend.

Mexican bean bake, potatoes choreadas

KHITCHRI

The origin of kedgeree, which we eat for breakfast, made with smoked haddock, boiled eggs and rice, goes back to an Indian dish known as *Khitchri*, which is a mixture of rice and dhal or lentils. It's a great staple dish, eaten all over India from the Nepalese north to the Sri Lankan south, and is made in many ways, with different kinds of dhal and indeed with a variety of kinds of rice. It can, of course, have all kinds of other additions to it, which is probably where the boiled eggs and smoked haddock came in. This simple version has a really good flavour. Eat it with chutneys, yoghurt, vegetable salads or, for grander meals, with a vegetable curry.

450 g (1 lb) Basmati rice
1 onion, peeled and finely chopped
30 ml (2 tbs) oil or ghee (see Ingredients, page 6)
5 ml (1 tsp) ground ginger
2.5 ml (¹/₂ tsp) cardamom seeds

5 ml (1 tsp) garam masala
225 g (8 oz) lentils (small orange ones or chana dhal – see Ingredients, page 5)
salt and pepper
15 ml (1 tbs) chopped coriander or parsley

Wash the rice 2 or 3 times in changes of cold water and put it to soak in warm water for about half an hour. Fry the onion in the ghee until soft, add the ginger, cardamom seeds and garam masala; stir together for 1 minute. Add the lentils and stir. Put in 2 cups of water, bring to the boil and simmer for 10 minutes if using the orange lentils, or 20 minutes if using chana dhal. Drain the rice and stir it into the mixture, adding 450 ml (⅘ pint) of water; season with salt and pepper and bring to the boil. Cover and turn down to the lowest possible heat. Cook for 15 minutes, then turn the heat off and, without removing the lid, leave to stand for another 10–15 minutes. To serve, turn out into a large serving dish and sprinkle with the coriander or parsley.

POTATO STUFFED PARATHAS

This dish was taught to me by my Aunt Abeda. Like so many Indian women of her generation, she had an amazing gift for handling bread and dough mixtures effortlessly to produce perfectly shaped and totally uniform puris, parathas and chapatis. My hands are much clumsier but the technique is easy enough to follow. I usually make the dough in a food processor, but you can make it by hand, kneading the dry ingredients and bonding them together gently before adding the water. This sort of food is eaten as a snack in Bangladesh, India and Pakistan but I think makes a marvellous vegetarian meal on its own, especially for a simple supper. Serve them with some chutney, some of the Prawn Balichow that's sold in supermarkets and speciality stores, and perhaps raita.

225 g (8 oz) Attar flour (see Ingredients, page 5) or 100 g (4 oz) plain white bread and 100 g (4 oz) fine-ground wholemeal flour
5 ml (1 tsp) salt
50 g (2 oz) butter, cut into small pieces
1 bunch spring onions, trimmed and chopped

2.5 ml (¹/₂ tsp) each turmeric, ground coriander, ground cumin, ground ginger
225 g (8 oz) potatoes, peeled and cut into fine dice
salt and pepper
30 ml (2 tbs) ghee (optional)

Into the food processor put the flour, salt and butter, and process briefly. Add 2–3 tablespoons of water (different flours absorb different amounts of water) and process in 2 or 3 bursts of 2–3 seconds. You should have a ball of quite soft dough at the end of this. If the mixture is still crumbly add a little more water very sparingly and process again; the dough will turn quite suddenly into a ball. Take the ball of dough out, put it in a greased plastic bag and leave to rest for half an hour. Meanwhile put the butter in a small pan, add the onions and spices, and fry for 5 minutes. Add the potatoes and just enough water to cover. Season and cook over a high heat until the potatoes are cooked through and the mixture is quite dry. It should be about the consistency of mashed potato but still have some texture left in it. Divide the dough up into 8 pieces and, taking each ball into your hands, work it into a small disc about the size of your palm. Take a tablespoon of the potato mixture and put this into the centre of the disc, closing up the outer edges to form a little bag. Give the top a twist to make sure it stays sealed, and put it aside. Do the same with all 8 balls of dough. On a well-floured surface, using a well-floured rolling pin, roll them out into discs slightly larger than a saucer. Heat a large non-stick or heavy cast iron frying pan until really hot and put the dry paratha onto it, pressing down gently with a spatula. If your pan is big enough you might be able to cook 2 at a time. Let it cook for about 4–5 minutes quite gently, without burning. Turn over and cook the other side. The bread should have a slightly speckled and brownish appearance. You can at this stage, if you wish, spread a little ghee on top of the paratha. Pile on a warm plate, separating the parathas with greaseproof paper.

POTATOES CHOREADAS

All over South America potatoes are cooked in interesting ways. This is really no surprise because potatoes were first developed in the highlands of South America, in territories controlled by the Incas in what is now Peru and Columbia. And the ingredient they most like to combine with potatoes these days is one that didn't exist in pre-Columbian America, cheese. This particular dish is a very simple one to make and is absolutely delicious as a supper dish with something green or fruity to follow it. The cheese used would usually be goat- or sheep's-milk based cheese, but Lancashire or Cheddar cheese will do very well for flavour.

1 kg (2 lb) potatoes
1 large onion, peeled and chopped
400 g (14 oz) tin Italian chopped tomatoes
or 450 g (1 lb) large ripe tomatoes, skinned
and chopped

15 ml (1 tbs) oil or oil and butter
salt and pepper
140 ml (5 fl oz) whipping cream
150 g (6 oz) grated cheese

This is usually made with potatoes in their skins but if the skin is particularly coarse or damaged, peel the potatoes before boiling them until tender but not at all crumbly. Sauté the onions and tomatoes in oil, or a mixture of oil and butter, until the onions are transparent. Season generously, add the cream and bring gently to the boil. Allow to simmer for a couple of minutes, then add the grated cheese and stir until it melts and forms a smooth sauce with the onions and tomatoes. Cut the boiled potatoes into pieces about the size of a walnut, put them into a serving dish and pour the sauce over. Although it's not traditional, I like to flash this under the grill so the sauce takes on a golden tinge here and there.

PROVISION BALL

A marvellous name which comes from the Trinidad and Tobago description of the solid starchy vegetable that used to provide the main nourishment for the slaves who worked the sugar fields. 'Provision' could be yam or sweet potato or taro, also known as dasheen in Trinidad. The important thing was it had to be solid and rib-sticking, but it could be very boring too. This method of cooking adds a marvellous crunchy outside to the succulent centre. You can make these with a variety of ingredients but as sweet potatoes and some yams are very widely available in British supermarkets these days a mixture is nice. Serve with a spicy or sweet and sour sauce.

225 g (½ lb) each yam and sweet potatoes
50 g (2 oz) finely chopped onion
50 g (2 oz) plain flour

salt and pepper
oil for deep frying

Peel the yam and sweet potato, cut into 2.5 cm (1 in) cubes and boil them in salted water until they are soft, between 8–10 minutes. Drain thoroughly and mash. Add the chopped onion and season generously. Some people add a little butter at this stage but I don't think it's necessary. Divide it into 12 balls and roll them lightly in the flour. You can allow them to stand in the fridge for up to 6 hours after this point. When ready to eat, deep fry them in hot oil for 4–5 minutes until golden and crunchy on the outside.

CARIBBEAN EGG PLANT IN COCONUT MILK

An exotic gratin made of egg plants or aubergines and flavoured with those standards of the Tropics, lime juice and coconut milk. This makes a marvellous vegetarian dish in its own right or can be eaten with grilled meat or fish.

700 g (1½ lb) aubergines
15 ml (1 tbs) cooking oil
30 ml (2 tbs) shredded coconut
1 medium onion
2 cloves of garlic

4 tomatoes
1 fresh red chilli
250 ml (½ pint) coconut milk, fresh or tinned
5 ml (1 tsp) salt
juice of 1 lime

Peel and quarter the onion, peel the garlic cloves and de-seed the chilli. Slice the aubergines and fry them lightly in the oil. Roughly chop the tomatoes and put them into a food processor with the onion, garlic, 4 or 5 tablespoons of the coconut milk, the lime juice, chilli and salt. Whizz until blended, then stir in the rest of the coconut milk. Butter a gratin dish and put in a layer of aubergine slices, season and follow with a layer of the coconut milk mix. Continue until you have used it all up, ending with a layer of the fried aubergines. Bake in a medium oven, 350°F/180°C/160 Fan/Gas mark 4/bottom of an Aga roasting oven, for 30 minutes. Sprinkle the shredded coconut over the top and bake for another 10 minutes until the top is crisp.

PLANTAINS IN CHEESE SAUCE

Plantains are large cooking bananas. They are about twice the size of an ordinary banana and are never eaten raw, even when they are fully ripe. They do however cook wonderfully, having a slightly more dense texture than dessert bananas and suiting savoury dishes particularly well. This comes from the Eastern Caribbean, the area of Barbados, Trinidad and Tobago, and is a marvellous combination of local ingredients and the cooking style of the colonial planters who have been resident in the islands for centuries.

4–5 plantains
375 ml (³⁄₄ pint) of milk
30 ml (2 tbs) butter
30 ml (2 tbs) plain flour

pinch of nutmeg
1 small chilli pepper
100 g (4 oz) grated cheese (preferably Lancashire)
seasoning

Use a little of the butter (no more than 15 ml (1 tbs)) to grease a baking dish. Peel the plantains and slice each across the grain into about 4 pieces. Neatly arrange them in the dish and season generously with salt and pepper. To make the cheese sauce, whisk the flour and the remaining butter into the milk and gently bring to the boil, whisking as you go. As it comes to the boil the sauce should become thick and glossy. Add the nutmeg. Season with salt but not pepper. Split the chilli pepper and remove the seeds. Chop it finely and add to the sauce. Then add about half of the grated cheese, about 50 g (2 oz). Pour the mixture over the plantains and sprinkle with the rest of the cheese. Put in the middle of a hot oven, 375°F/190°C/Gas mark 5. Cook for about 35 minutes until the sauce is golden brown. This is delicious on its own, or with chops or fried fish.

Japanese food – miso soup, sashimi, chicken yakitori, sukiyaki, noodles, sushi rice, pickled vegetables, spinach with sesame seed dressing

VEGETABLES

Vegetables, more than anything else, symbolize profusion and abundance for me. My most vivid food memories are of vegetables being picked or bought, or piled high in rich profusion. These memories are brought to life by markets like the one at Papeen in the foothills of the Blue Mountains in Jamaica. Every Saturday morning, in the years we lived there, began with a trip to the market at Papeen. Rows and rows of countrywomen brought their produce in from small holdings and farms, heaps of shining vegetables and fruit, some familiar, and some extremely unfamiliar, and spent the time bargaining, joking, feeling and weighing. I learned more about West Indian cooking in those sunlit mornings from those cheerful women than from any books or formal teaching. I can also remember the extraordinary markets of Dhaka and Delhi, with fruit, vegetables and spices piled high, in brilliant colours and enormous quantities. The markets of Singapore, great cavernous halls provided by the municipality, are where the street sellers and stall holders gather in riotous proximity. I watched as people buying vegetables had them cleaned and prepared in a way that would astonish a Western greengrocer – the garlic peeled, the spring onions trimmed, the salads washed – real convenience food if I ever saw it.

I have vivid memories of astonishing vegetables from gardens in Cape Province in South Africa: fresh carrots, turnips, beetroot, cabbage so sweet it tasted like apples, sold from the back of a farm lorry. And I remember picking the spiky bitter gourds that form an important part of indigenous Indian cookery, in the garden of one of my cousins in Bangladesh. Individual dishes bring back memories too: aubergines turning into the most wonderful garlicky and olive oil dips in Turkey; and an Indian dish of spinach flavoured with lemon; an incredible tempura in the hills below Mount Fuji in Japan, made entirely from wild produce gathered from the autumn forest by the abbot of a Buddhist monastery.

There is no doubt that vegetables make the most wonderful food and, in addition to our everyday British vegetables, which can be cooked in myriad ways, more exotic vegetables can now easily be found in our shops and supermarkets. I have included some of my favourite vegetable dishes in this chapter: I hope you'll enjoy them.

BROCCOLI WITH OYSTER SAUCE

Broccoli is supposed to be the most popular vegetable in America even though the Republican President George Bush, didn't much like it. He might if he tasted this way of cooking it, which comes out of the Chinese tradition of vegetable cooking. It's very simple and surprisingly substantial. It won't work with frozen broccoli, at least not in my experience, but fresh broccoli is available nearly all the year round these days. No one in China would dream of making their own oyster sauce but you have to buy good quality sauce to make this dish. Make sure by looking at the label that there were real oysters involved in the making of it. It's like a very thick and savoury soy sauce with only a hint of fish in it, rather like our Worcester sauce with its hint of anchovies. Serve this dish as part of a Chinese meal, to provide both texture and savour.

30 ml (2 tbs) oil
1 cm (¹/₂ in) piece fresh root ginger, peeled and finely chopped
1 clove garlic, peeled and finely chopped
450 g (1 lb) fresh green broccoli, washed and cut into small florets

2.5 ml (¹/₂ tsp) salt
90 ml (6 tbs) (half a cup) water
90 ml (6 tbs) oyster sauce (see Ingredients, page 6)

Put the oil in a wok or a deep frying pan and heat it. Add the garlic and ginger for just 30 seconds, then put in the broccoli. Stir fry it, tossing and turning it regularly but carefully until it goes a dark bright green. Sprinkle with the salt and, over the maximum heat, pour in the water and cover for one minute, allowing the water to boil and steam the broccoli so it's cooked right through. Take the lid off and allow the water to evaporate – this should take no more than 2 minutes in total. When the broccoli is thoroughly cooked, tip it into a serving dish which just holds it, pour the oyster sauce into the cooking liquid, stir quickly to heat through, and pour over the cooked broccoli.

AUBERGINES IMAM BAYELDI

Literally translated, this famous Middle Eastern dish means that the Imam (or local religious leader) fainted. There's often dispute about why. Some say because the sheer deliciousness of the dish overwhelmed him, and others because the incredible expense of the ingredients caused him to panic. My inclination is towards the first explanation, not least because aubergines are known in the Middle East as the caviare of the poor – they're not an expensive or exotic vegetable but an everyday one. This is a delicious way of eating them and can be consumed hot or cold. If cold, choose small aubergines that will allow a complete half each; they make a wonderful first course. If you're eating them hot you can sub-divide them, but try them as a course on their own either way, because the flavours are so delicious and sophisticated that it's a pity to mix them with anything.

1 large or 2 medium aubergines (weighing approximately 500–700 g (1–1½ lb))
salt
1 clove garlic, peeled and finely chopped
half a large or 1 small onion, peeled and finely chopped
90 ml (6 tbs) olive oil
225 g (8 oz) chopped tomatoes
15 ml (1 tbs) tomato purée

pinch chilli powder
pinch dried thyme
5 ml (1 tsp) dried basil
freshly ground black pepper
50 g (2 oz) chopped parsley or fresh green coriander
25 g (1 oz) pine nuts
juice of half a lemon (optional)

Cut the aubergines in half lengthwise and score the cut flesh deeply with a knife. Sprinkle with a tablespoon of salt, put in a colander and drain for 30 minutes to an hour. Fry the onion and garlic in 2 tablespoons of the oil, until translucent. Add the tomatoes, the tomato purée and the herbs (except for the parsley or coriander). Season and simmer for 10 minutes. You may find the mixture needs a pinch of sugar to bring out its full flavour. When the aubergines have drained (this removes some of their bitter liquid), rinse them to remove the excess salt and, in a large frying pan, add 2 more tablespoons of the olive oil and fry them gently on both sides for 10 minutes. Take them out and place them in a baking dish into which they will fit neatly. Spread the tomato mixture on the cut sides, making sure that it goes into the gaps and slits, and drizzle the remaining olive oil over the aubergines and tomato mixture. Spread half the finely chopped parsley or coriander and all the pine nuts on top and bake in a medium oven (180°C, 350°F, Gas mark 4) for 30 minutes until thoroughly cooked. Sprinkle the rest of the fresh herbs on to the aubergine slices before serving. If you're serving them cold, allow them to cool in their own juices and, before serving, squeeze the juice of half a lemon over them.

AUBERGINE FRITTERS

This very simple dish is eaten in many different countries of the world. It's eaten in Indonesia as part of a Rijstaeffel; it's eaten in the Middle East as part of a Mezze; in Japan as part of a Tempura; and all over South America and the West Indies in its own right. You can add flavour or savour to these fritters in any of those regional styles – soy sauce dips for Japanese, tomato *salsu* for South America (see page 226), a squeeze of lemon and a little houmous for the Middle East. Whichever way they are served, they're quite delicious and incredibly easy to make.

700 g (1½ lb) large aubergines
cooking oil (see method below)
60 ml (4 tbs) flour

2.5 ml (½ tsp) ground bay leaves
2.5 ml (½ tsp) paprika
2.5 ml (½ tsp) garlic salt

Slice the aubergines at an angle across the grain into slices approximately 5 mm (¼ in) thick. With the aubergines now available in this country, salting and draining for this particular recipe isn't necessary, so heat enough oil in a large frying pan, into which the aubergines will fit comfortably, to a depth of about 2–5 mm (⅛–¼ in). You can suit the oil to the style in which you're going to eat them – olive for the Middle East, corn for the South American style or soya oil for the Far East. Mix the flour and the herbs together. Dip the fritters in this and slide them carefully into the hot oil. They will need about 2–3 minutes a side and should be golden brown when you turn them. After 2–3 minutes on the second side, slide them onto kitchen paper to drain. Eat them quickly – they don't improve with keeping. This is the sort of dish I like to serve in the kitchen, with people eating them as they come out of the pan.

THREE-FRIED DELICIOUS

This mushroom dish exploits the Chinese love of both dried and fresh mushrooms. You can buy a wide variety of dried mushrooms in any Chinese supermarket. The two kinds I'm suggesting here are Woodears, which is a variety eaten almost entirely for its texture, and Cepes, or *porcini* as they are known in Italy, which are included for their flavour. In addition, there are some fresh mushrooms called Shitake which are now quite widely available in Britain – this is a Japanese-style mushroom grown on oak logs which has both a firm texture and a delicious flavour. If you can't find the specific kinds of mushroom named here, try and find three different varieties of mushrooms, at least one of them being dried. Dried mushrooms are expensive but you don't need a lot: when they're soaked they swell extraordinarily and have a very intense flavour.

50 g (2 oz) dried weight Woodears
50 g (2 oz) dried weight Cepes
150 g (6 oz) fresh Shitake mushrooms (or chestnut or conventional British mushrooms), trimmed
cooking oil
1 stalk celery, trimmed and finely chopped

4 stalks spring onion, trimmed and finely chopped
2.5 ml (½ tsp) salt
60 ml (4 tbs) soy sauce
5 ml (1 tsp) sugar
10 ml (1 dsp) cornflour

Soak the dried mushrooms for at least 15 minutes and preferably an hour in warm water. They will expand enormously. Take out of the soaking water, making sure that they are free of all grit. Strain the soaking water and keep it. Slice both dried and fresh mushrooms into 1 cm (½ in) strips. Put 2 tablespoons of cooking oil into a wok or deep frying pan and fry the celery and spring onions in it for 1 minute. Add the mushrooms and toss and stir fry for 2 minutes. Add a cup of the soaking liquid, the salt, soy sauce and sugar, and bring to the boil. Stir the cornflour into a couple of tablespoonfuls of the mushroom soaking liquid and stir that into the sauce to thicken it. Bring it gently to the boil and check for seasoning before serving. The combination of textures and flavours is delicious.

Three-fried delicious

GREEN BEANS WITH GARLIC

This Chinese-style vegetable goes extremely well with a lot of European, particularly Mediterranean-type, meat and fish dishes. I first came across it in a Chinese restaurant in London's Soho, alas no longer with us since the gentrification of the area, but the dish was so delicious that I asked for the recipe. You need the very thin shoelace-type green beans for this one.

15 ml (1 tbs) each cooking oil and butter
450 g (1 lb) thin green beans, trimmed
2 cloves garlic, peeled and roughly chopped

15 ml (1 tbs) soy sauce
pinch sugar
1 cup water

Heat the oil and butter in a saucepan with a close-fitting lid. When the butter has melted and stopped sizzling, add the beans and toss them, then cover the pan, turning the heat down to low for 3 minutes. Add the garlic to the beans with the soy sauce, sugar and water. Bring to the boil and allow the liquid to boil off. By the time it has vanished, the beans will be cooked through and impregnated with the flavour of the garlic. They should be glossy and bright green. Serve them in a hot dish quickly with the bits of garlic mixed in. These will no longer have the bite they once had, since their flavour has been taken into the beans.

TUNISIAN CARROT SALAD

This is often served at the beginning of a meal in Tunisia, with a tomato and green pepper salad on the side. It's eaten with slices of hot and crusty flat Arab bread and I'm often tempted into asking for a second helping of the first course, then not having any room left for the main dish which is to follow. The unusual spicing and the brilliant colour of these carrots makes them a marvellous addition to a North African or Middle Eastern Meal.

700 g (1½ lb) carrots, peeled and cut into cigarette-sized pieces
5 ml (1 tsp) salt
15 ml (1 tbs) white sugar
15 ml (1 tbs) olive oil

15 ml (1 tbs) lemon juice
30 ml (2 tbs) chopped fresh coriander or parsley
1.25 ml (¼ tsp) chilli powder
2.5 ml (½ tsp) paprika

Boil the carrots in a little water with a pinch of salt until just cooked but still retaining some crispness. Drain them and put all the remaining ingredients into the saucepan to heat up. Return the carrots and toss them quickly for 2 minutes over high heat until they are glazed and coated. Put them to one side to cool and serve them when they're cool but not chilled as part of an appetizer or salad buffet.

PEPPERS IN TOMATO SAUCE

This recipe is common all over the Middle East. It's a form of *ratatouille* that's particularly popular in Turkey and the northern parts of Asia Minor. It can be eaten spicy hot or very sweet, depending upon both your taste and the kind of peppers you put into it. You can eat it with other dishes as part of a vegetarian meal with something crisp like Falafel (page 223) and some hot pitta bread (page 177).

60 ml (4 tbs) olive oil
450 g (1 lb) red peppers, sweet or spicy (not chilli peppers), de-seeded and sliced into 5 mm (¼ in) rounds
450 g (1 lb) onions, peeled and thinly sliced
5 ml (1 tsp) salt

400 g (14 oz) tin Italian-style chopped tomatoes (or very ripe Mediterranean tomatoes, sliced)
5 ml (1 tsp) sugar
15 ml (1 tbs) tomato purée
juice of half a lemon
15 ml (1 tbs) chopped parsley

Heat the oil in a large, heavy-based saucepan and fry the peppers in it gently until their skins go wrinkly and soft. Add the onions and fry those till they're translucent. Add the fresh or tinned tomatoes, the salt and sugar, and simmer for 15–20 minutes. Add the tomato purée and the lemon juice, check for seasoning, and simmer for another 10–15 minutes until the vegetables are all soft but not disintegrated. Pile into a serving dish and sprinkle with the chopped parsley, some of which can be stirred through the mixture if you prefer. This dish can be eaten hot or cold, in which case a little more lemon juice will probably improve it.

Peppers in tomato sauce, falafel, pitta bread

POTATOES WITH FENNEL SEEDS

Madhur Jaffrey taught me this recipe during a filming session we did together for exotic Christmas dishes some years ago, in Birmingham of all places. Madhur is not only a great cook, television personality and cookery writer, but she's also, in India, a great film star – a sort of cross between Meryl Streep and Faye Dunaway. On the streets of Birmingham she was stopped, not because of her television series on cookery but to get the signature of a real luminary of the Indian cinema. This recipe is incredibly easy and has a stunning flavour. Madhur would say it wasn't strictly Indian but the principles and the flavourings are.

1 kg (2 lb) potatoes, scrubbed
60 ml (4 tbs) vegetable oil (not olive)
5 ml (1 tsp) fennel seeds

5 ml (1 tsp) paprika
1.25 ml (¼ tsp) cayenne pepper
salt and black pepper

Boil the potatoes until just cooked. You can peel them at this point if you wish, but either way cut them in half, or if they're very large into quarters. Heat the oil in a large frying pan until it's just below smoking. Add the fennel seeds and then immediately add the potatoes. This will reduce the heat of the oil but they should be cooked over a medium flame from now on. Fry them until one side is browned then tilt them over until the other side is also browned. Mix together the paprika and cayenne pepper and sprinkle over the potatoes, then cook for another minute. Drain them on absorbent paper, season with salt and black pepper and serve immediately as part of a meal or as a quite delicious first course in their own right. Do try some raita (page 225) with this.

Variation You can substitue for the fennel seeds, 10 ml (2 tsp) whole cumin seeds and 5 ml (1 tsp) black mustard seeds, substituting 1.25 ml (¼ tsp) turmeric for the cayenne pepper.

Potatoes with fennel seeds, sag dhal, raita (top); Bhindi bhaji (bottom)

ALOO GOBI

This mixture of potatoes and cauliflower is very popular all over India. There are many variations of it, some with thick rich sauces, some with vivid spicing. My favourite version is this, which has all the flavour but not too much pungency.

450 g (1 lb) potatoes, peeled and cut into walnut-sized pieces
1 small head cauliflower (weighing approximately 450 g/1 lb), broken into florets
30 ml (2 tbs) ghee or vegetable oil

1 large onion, peeled and finely chopped
2 cloves garlic, peeled and finely sliced
2.5 ml (½ tsp) mustard seed
1.25 ml (¼ tsp) cayenne or chilli pepper
15 ml (1 tbs) garam masala
juice of a lemon

Boil the potatoes for 6–8 minutes until starting to be tender but not cooked through. Break the cauliflower into florets and add to the potatoes as they come to the boil. Cook for another 5 minutes. At the end of cooking, both vegetables should still retain a little crispness. Drain and, in the same saucepan, heat the ghee or vegetable oil. Add the onion and garlic to the saucepan and fry till light gold. Add the mustard seeds and turn the heat up high until the seeds start to pop. Put in the cayenne pepper, then add the potatoes and cauliflower, and half a cup of water, and turn gently so that the vegetables are mixed with the onions and spice mixture. Simmer until the liquid is evaporated and the potatoes and vegetables are frying gently. Sprinkle with the garam masala, squeeze the lemon juice over, then turn off the heat and allow to stand for 2–3 minutes before serving.

LEMON SAG

This is a copy of a spiced spinach dish that I have eaten all over the sub-continent but have to say that I think is best cooked in a small restaurant in Streatham High Road in South London. In India all kinds of different green vegetables go under the name of *sag*, although we normally translate it as spinach in Britain. For this recipe then you can use real spinach or what's called perpetual spinach, or even the green leaves of the vegetable known as Swiss chard or the New Zealand spinach which grows well in hot summers. This dish is quickly cooked and its delicate taste makes it a marvellous vegetable dish to go with rice and one of the drier meat curries.

1 kg (2 lb) fresh spinach or similar leaves, trimmed
30 ml (2 tbs) ghee or vegetable oil
1 clove garlic, peeled and chopped
salt

5 ml (1 tsp) each cumin seeds and garam masala
juice and grated rind of a lemon
2.5 ml (¹/₂ tsp) white sugar

Blanch the spinach leaves in a saucepan full of boiling water for just 1 minute. Drain and roughly chop them in the colander so all the excess liquid runs out. In a saucepan, heat the ghee and add the garlic and cumin seeds until they turn golden brown (about 2 minutes). Add the spinach and turn in the hot oil, seasoning generously with salt. Add the garam masala, the lemon juice and its grated rind, and allow to cook for 2–3 minutes, turning regularly. At the end of that time add the sugar, turn again, turn off the heat, and leave to stand for 2–3 minutes for the flavours to balance. Serve hot.

SAG DHAL

This is a lovely, gently flavoured dish that I like to eat on its own just with rice, but it also goes very well as part of a grander sub-continental meal. It can be served, for example, with kebabs or grilled spiced meat and some Indian breads; these are often used as a kind of spoon to eat dhal when it's not too runny and liquid. This dish also looks pretty, the golden colour of the lentils marbled with the dark green of the spinach.

30 ml (2 tbs) oil or ghee
1 onion, peeled and chopped
1 clove garlic, peeled and chopped
5 ml (1 tsp) turmeric
2.5 ml (¹/₂ tsp) chilli powder
225 g (8 oz) lentils – split yellow chana dhal or orange lentils, rinsed

salt and black pepper
450 g (1 lb) fresh spinach leaves, washed and trimmed and cut into 1 cm (¹/₂ in) strips
10 ml (1 dsp) amchoor (see Ingredients, page 5)

Heat the ghee in a saucepan and fry the onion and garlic gently for 2 minutes. Add the turmeric, chilli powder and the lentils. Cover generously with water to come at least 2.5 cm (1 in) over the lentils, bring to the boil and simmer till the lentils are soft (20 minutes for orange lentils, 35 minutes for yellow chana dhal). Season generously with salt and black pepper and add the spinach. Bring to the boil and turn down to a simmer for another 10 minutes, until the spinach has had a chance to cook with the dhal. Stir thoroughly and add the amchoor, which is used to add a slightly sour and fruity note to dhal dishes all over the sub-continent.

BHINDI BHAJI

Bhindi are okra, or lady's fingers as they are often known — small, slightly glutinous green beans that are one of India's staple vegetables. Okra is also widely found in the southern United States, where it is used to make the classic dishes of Gumbo, as well as all through the West Indies and South America. This is a particularly pleasant way of eating it which will certainly go with dishes from all the above-mentioned areas. Okra is now widely available in supermarkets and better greengrocers; it's quite an expensive vegetable but you don't need much to produce a lot of flavour and texture.

225 g (8 oz) okra
cooking oil
1 large onion, peeled and thinly sliced
2 cloves garlic, peeled and crushed
2.5 ml (½ tsp) each turmeric, chilli powder
and ground ginger

400 g (14 oz) tin Italian tomatoes (or very ripe, fresh tomatoes), chopped small
salt and pepper
5 ml (1 tsp) lemon juice
5 ml (1 tsp) brown sugar

Trim the okra by cutting off the stem and tip and cutting each one in half across. Heat 2 tablespoons of oil in a deep saucepan, add the onion and garlic and the spices and fry gently for 2–3 minutes. Add the tomatoes and a cupful of water. Bring to the boil and simmer for 10 minutes. Add the okra, season generously and cook over a low heat for 20 minutes until the vegetables are soft. You may need to add a little more water to it, but don't make the sauce too liquid. When it's cooked, season with the lemon juice and sugar, checking as you add them for balance. The sauce should have a slightly sweet and sour flavour.

BENGALI BHUNA CHANA

This is one of the classic dishes of eastern India, made with chick peas. It is a substantial dish that's often eaten as a main course in its own right, and it has a delicious dry but savoury sauce. The recipe can have potato cubes added to it for extra bulk and flavour and I have also had it with chopped green and red peppers to produce a very different and slightly crisp texture.

225 g (8 oz) chick peas, soaked for 6 hours
30 ml (2 tbs) oil
2 onions, peeled and sliced
2 cloves garlic, peeled and sliced
2.5 ml (½ tsp) chilli powder

5 ml (1 tsp) each ground coriander, cumin, ginger, turmeric and garam masala
2.5 ml (½ tsp) chilli powder
1 cup tamarind water
salt and pepper
10 ml (1 dsp) soft brown sugar

Put the chick peas into a casserole, cover them to about 2.5 cm (1 in) above with water, and put them in a medium oven (180°C, 350°F, Gas mark 4) for 1½–2 hours until they are cooked through. Drain them, retaining the liquid. In a saucepan put the oil, the sliced onions and garlic and all the spices except the garam masala. Fry for 3 or 4 minutes until the spices are fragrant and the onions and garlic translucent. Add the chick peas and the tamarind water, or lemon juice and ⅔ cup of the cooking water from the chick peas. Season generously, bring to the boil and simmer at a fast rate until the liquid is almost evaporated. Sprinkle on the garam masala and the sugar, stir and leave to stand for 2–3 minutes. Check that the balance of the sauce is right; it may need a little more lemon juice or salt, or a little more liquid from the cooking water to produce a thick, coating sauce with a hint of sweetness as well as a sharp lemony bite.

POTATO CAKES

Potato cakes are eaten all over the world in an enormous range of variations. I have given just two versions here to show how varied and delicious they can be – exotically spiced Indonesian Pergardel, and Llanputas from the home of the potato, in Peru. Both start with the same basic ingredients and preparation, then vary afterwards.

700 g (1½ lb) potatoes, peeled and cut into
even-sized pieces
1 onion, peeled and finely chopped

30 ml (2 tbs) oil
1 egg

Boil the potatoes until they are cooked through but not watery. Fry the onion in the oil until it's translucent. Mash the potatoes, add the onion and beat in the egg. At this point you proceed differently according to the dish.

Pergadel

100 g (4 oz) minced beef
15 ml (1 tbs) oil
5 ml (1 tsp) cumin seeds

1 bunch spring onions, trimmed and
chopped
2.5 ml (½ tsp) ground cinnamon

Fry the beef in the oil until it's well browned and add to the potato mixture. Add the spring onions, and stir in the spices. With dampened hands, form into 8 balls and flatten them a little so that they resemble slightly fat hamburger shapes. Fry them either in deep oil or in 5 mm (¼ in) oil in a large frying pan until brown on both sides.

Llanputas

2.5 ml (½ tsp) turmeric
pinch allspice
salt and pepper

100 g (4 oz) cheese, (Cheddar, Lancashire
or Wensleydale), grated
cooking oil

Stir the allspice and turmeric into the mashed potatoes, then add the seasoning and grated cheese. Divide into 12 portions, and form them into quite flat cakes with your hands. Flour these lightly if you like before frying them in hot oil until crisp brown on both sides.

BAKED SWEET POTATOES

Sweet potatoes, or Louisiana Yams as they are known in the southern United States, come in a range of knobbly sizes and two colours: white fleshed and orange. There is a great debate about which are the best tasting. My vote is clearly for the orange kind, sometimes known as pumpkin potatoes in Jamaica, but both are delicious and widely available throughout the year now in Britain. I've given a couple of recipes for them but one of my favourite ways is the simplest one, which is to bake them and eat them with butter and a little cinnamon and sugar. This is a form of the candied sweet potato that's much beloved in America at Thanksgiving time. One of the reasons why sweet potatoes have taken a long time to catch on in Britain is that in the Second World War a lot of them were used to feed troops. Army cooks weren't quite sure what to do with them, and I have to say that few things make worse chips. If you do get a chance to try them, don't miss it. They are one of the most pleasurable of all tropical vegetables.

2 sweet potatoes, weighing approximately
225 g (8 oz) each
50 g (2 oz) butter

10 ml (1 dsp) caster sugar
pinch cinnamon
salt and pepper

Scrub the sweet potatoes and trim them carefully with a sharp knife. Put to bake in a medium oven (180°C, 350°F, Gas mark 4) on a baking tray for approximately 45–50 minutes. Test with a skewer to make sure they are cooked through. Split them lengthwise and spread with the butter, then sprinkle with the sugar and the cinnamon; put back in the oven for 5 minutes to allow the butter and spices to melt. Serve, with salt and pepper to be added according to taste.

SWEET POTATOES WITH TANGERINE

This is a recipe from the southern part of Africa where sweet potatoes are a major staple crop. It uses tangerine peel to flavour them but you can use orange peel as well with a similar, though slightly different, result. This is nice as part of a vegetarian meal, served with three or four other dishes.

700 g (1½ lb) sweet potatoes
30 ml (2 tbs) butter
15 ml (1 tbs) demerara sugar

5 ml (1 tsp) ground ginger
peel from 1 tangerine or half an orange
(pith removed), cut into matchstick pieces

Peel the sweet potatoes and keep them in slightly acidulated water (a dash of lemon juice does fine) to stop them going brown. Cut them into 2.5 cm (1 in) sections and boil in salted water for approximately 15 minutes until tender. Drain them, melt the butter in the saucepan they were cooked in and put the potatoes back in with the sugar, ginger and the tangerine peel. Toss gently to mix, and leave over a low heat for 5 minutes before serving.

FRIED PLANTAIN

This is one of the traditional side dishes for Jamaican food and indeed it is enormously popular all over the West Indies and South America. Plantains are rather like giant bananas, both to look at and in their cooked taste. They are not good to eat raw, however, as their capacity to pucker the mouth is second only to that of lemons or unripe persimmons. They are used to make porridge, cut into fine chips, or can be added to bulk up a casserole, especially when cooked in their green state. In their unripe state they are also supposed to be very beneficial for preventing and helping to treat stomach ulcers, but when they're really ripe they are most delicious cooked like this.

2 plantains
60 ml (4 tbs) seasoned flour

60 ml (4 tbs) oil
5 ml (1 tsp) salt

Peel the plantains as you would a banana and cut diagonally across the grain into 5 mm (¼ in) slices. Dust them with the flour and fry them in hot oil to a depth of 5 mm (¼ in) for 3–4 minutes on each side until they go brown. Drain them and salt after cooking. They have a nutty sweet flavour that complements a whole range of dishes.

HUNAAN CARROTS IN PEANUT SAUCE

This Chinese recipe never ceases to surprise people used to the stir fry Cantonese style of cooking. The carrots, cut in a special way, are spiced quite significantly and sauced very richly. This is a substantial dish for cold weather eating and makes a really pleasant addition to a regional Chinese meal, made up of several dishes.

700 g (1½ lb) carrots, peeled
2.5 ml (½ tsp) star anise (see Ingredients,
page 6)
60 ml (4 tbs) peanut butter

1 cup water
15 ml (1 tbs) soy sauce
2.5 ml (½ tsp) chilli powder
salt and pepper

Cut the carrots into triangular chunks. This is done by putting the carrot down horizontally across in front of you and holding the knife at 45° so that you cut the carrot on the bias. When you've made one cut, roll the carrot towards you through 90° so that the cut surface is pointing upwards, and cut again on the same bias. Continue doing this all the way down the carrot and you will wind up with triangular shaped pieces of carrot which have the advantage of providing maximum surface area for quick cooking. It also means that they cook at an even rate. It's the classic Chinese way of cutting carrots and looks as pretty as it is efficient. Put the carrots in just enough water to cover them and add the star anise, which you can if you like crush a little for an even more intense flavour. Salt the water, bring them to the boil and cook till the carrots are just tender, about 10–12 minutes. Drain them and, in the same saucepan, add the peanut butter, the water, the soy sauce, and the chilli powder. Bring to the boil and stir until the sauce turns thick and shiny. Add the carrots and check for seasoning before serving.

GARLIC CHILLI CABBAGE

Here is a Chinese dish which has been adopted all over South East Asia, with some variants. You can make it with almost any kind of cabbage – it's equally successful with one of the crisp Dutch ones normally sold for coleslaw, or one of the Chinese-style pale green celery cabbages. It also works with the crinkly coarse-leaved savoys we get in the winter. Adjust the volume of chilli and garlic to your own taste and to balance the strength of the cabbage's flavour. The important thing is to make sure that the leaves are still crisp and have some bite to them after cooking.

700 g (1½ lb) crisp cabbage
30 ml (2 tbs) oil
2 cloves garlic, peeled and crushed

15 ml (1 tbs) Chinese-style chilli sauce
2.5 ml (½ tsp) salt

Shred the cabbage across the grain into 5 mm (¼ in) slices, removing any core or solid pieces. Heat the oil in a wok or a large frying pan, add the garlic and fry for 30 seconds, then add the cabbage. Stir and toss for 2 minutes until the cabbage is coated with the garlic oil and is beginning to soften. Add the chilli sauce and half a cup of water. Cover for 30 seconds for the cabbage to steam. Season and serve immediately. There should be very little liquid left in the bottom, and what there is should *not* be served with the cabbage.

PUMPKIN PLUGS

Pumpkin is one of the most popular vegetables throughout the Tropics and is cooked in a wide variety of ways. Not many of these however have what you might call an elegance of form. That's not true of this recipe which is both simple and highly attractive to look at as well as eat. It's best served as an accompanying vegetable to fish or poultry dishes.

700 g (1½ lb) pumpkin or butternut squash
50 g (2 oz) butter

2.5 ml (½ tsp) nutmeg
seasoning

De-seed the pumpkin or, if you're using butternut squash, split it and de-seed that. Scrub the skin and then, using an apple corer, working from the skin side, remove plugs of the pumpkin which should be about 2.5–4 cm (1 in–1½ in) long and about the thickness of a medium cigar. When you've removed all the plugs you can, put them into a steamer or colander over a saucepan of boiling water and steam for 12–15 minutes. When they're cooked the colour is entrancing, ranging from gold at the pumpkin end and through pale green to dark green at the skin side. Mix the butter and nutmeg and salt and pepper together and toss the pumpkin in the seasoned butter before serving.

SWEET POTATO PANCAKES

The origin of these pancakes is a bit shrouded in mystery. I first came across them in the USA associated with soul food, or Southern cooking, but I suspect that originally they came from rather further South than even the state of Louisiana. They are very easy to make and delicious with chicken or beef dishes that have a little spicy gravy.

225 g (8 oz) sweet potatoes, peeled
2 spring onions
25 g (1 oz) self raising flour

1 egg
30 ml (2 tbs) milk
salt and pepper

Cut the sweet potato into 2.5 cm (1 in) cubes and boil in salted water until soft. This will take about 8–9 minutes. Meanwhile clean and finely chop the spring onion and beat the egg and mix with the milk. When the sweet potato is cooked, drain it and mash it thoroughly. Mix it with the chopped onion, the egg and milk and the tablespoon of flour until you have a soft dough or thick batter. Season generously and fry in a frying pan with a little vegetable oil, a tablespoon at a time. The mixture will flatten out into a pancake, helped occasionally with a spatula, and should be fried for 3 minutes on each side until golden brown.

GEMMA'S POTATO FRITTERS

There are many versions of potato fritters and potato cakes from all over the world. I first ate these in an extraordinary restaurant built into a tree on a Caribbean beach. It may have been the surroundings but it seemed to me, then and subsequently, that these were one of the nicest ways of cooking potato fritters that I have ever come across. The cook, whose name was Gemma, after some persuasion, divulged her simple recipe.

700 g (1½ lb) potatoes
100 g (4 oz) tomatoes
6 spring onions (scallions)

1 green pepper
2 eggs
salt and pepper

Peel and grate or shred the potatoes finely. Fine chop the tomatoes and trim and fine chop the onions and the pepper. Mix thoroughly with the potatoes, season generously and beat in the eggs. In its original form this was deep fried tablespoons at a time for about 4–5 minutes but can also be shallow fried in the same quantities, being turned after 3 minutes until both sides are crispy and golden and the insides still moist and slightly creamy.

MEXICAN-STYLE COURGETTES

Courgettes, like so many other vegetables, have a long history in Mexico going back nearly 5,000 years. It's extraordinary that it has taken us nearly 300 years of acquaintance to discover that marrows are best eaten in their baby state. I think it was Elizabeth David who transformed our appreciation of this vegetable back in the late '50s and early '60s, but I don't think even she was familiar with the way they are cooked in Mexico. There are, of course, many different ways but this one is my favourite. It's quite a sophisticated way of cooking courgettes, involving two separate processes, but it produces a very different result to the *ratatouille* style from the Mediterranean, although it uses some of the same ingredients.

450 g (1 lb) courgettes, washed and the ends trimmed off
30 ml (2 tbs) oil
15 ml (1 tbs) tomato purée

1 bunch spring onions, trimmed and finely chopped, including some green
salt and pepper
15 ml (1 tbs) chopped parsley

Peel the courgettes carefully with a potato peeler, leaving stripes of green along the edge of each stroke so that the courgette has a tiger-striped appearance. Cut the courgettes into 2.5 cm (1 in) pieces. Put some water into a steamer base or a saucepan over which you can put a fireproof colander. Bring it to the boil and steam the courgettes for 5 minutes. Heat the oil in a separate saucepan, add the spring onions when it is hot, then add the courgettes, and stir until coated with oil, and sizzling. Add the tomato purée, put the lid on the saucepan and shake vigorously two or three times so that the purée spreads around the courgettes. Take off the heat, check for seasoning, and serve with the parsley sprinkled over them.

Achar Achar

ACHAR ACHAR

I'm not sure whether this is really a salad or a pickle. It's eaten with South East Asian and Indonesian dishes and gives both a crunch and savour. The word *achar* is used in India to indicate a condiment or salted vegetable meant to be eaten as an accompaniment to the meal, rather like we would use chutney or mustard. So that's the origin, but Achar Achar is eaten rather more generously than that and often with one of the set meals you get in Malaysia and parts of Indonesia, with a plateful of rice and four or five goodies like Crisp Fried Chicken, Deep Fried Prawns and Spiced Peanuts around it. Achar Achar is one of the regular accompaniments that provides both colour and vegetable crunchiness. It can be made in quite generous quantities and kept in a sealed bowl, in the fridge for up to a week.

One quarter of a crisp coleslaw-type cabbage, shredded
100 g (4 oz) carrots, peeled and cut into matchstick pieces
3 celery sticks, trimmed and cut into long matchsticks
1 large onion, peeled and cut into thin rings
100 g (4 oz) string green beans, trimmed

5 ml (1 tsp) salt
225 g (8 oz) beansprouts, washed
30 ml (2 tbs) oil
5 ml (1 tsp) turmeric
2.5 ml (½ tsp) chilli powder
2.5 ml (½ tsp) lemon grass powder (see Ingredients, page 6)
30 ml (2 tbs) rice or cider vinegar
15 ml (1 tbs) white sugar

Put all the vegetables except the beansprouts into a pan, just cover with cold water, and bring to the boil. Take off the heat immediately. Add the salt and allow to stand for 10 minutes. Drain, then add the beansprouts. In the same empty pan, put the oil and the spices and heat gently until the spices become fragrant, about 2–3 minutes. Add the vegetables and turn them in the oil. Add the vinegar and sugar and bring to the boil. Cook for just 2 minutes and allow to cool. Pour the vegetables into a dish, preferably china or glass, making sure you put all the spices, vinegar and oil over them. Allow to stand for at least 6 hours before serving.

AVOCADO SALAD

Here is the recipe for the salad so often recommended with West Indian meals as it has a wonderfully refreshing and cooling effect.

2 avocados, carefully peeled and halved
2 handfuls of crisp lettuce leaves, washed and shredded into thin ribbons
juice of 1 lime (or small lemon)

30 ml (2 tbs) salad oil
5 ml (1 tsp) sugar
pinch salt

Place the avocados cut side down and slice them lengthwise into 5 mm (¼ in) slices. If you do this carefully, leaving the tip of the avocado uncut, you can then create 4 fans of sliced avocado by placing the cut fruit onto the lettuce and pressing slightly to spread the slices. Without any delay, mix the juice of the lime or lemon with the oil, sugar and pinch of salt; coat the avocado, sprinkling the remainder over the lettuce.

GADO GADO

The supreme salad of South East Asia, it's often eaten as a snack but it can form a full, light meal.

1 medium-sized lettuce or coleslaw-type cabbage, washed and shredded
225 g (8 oz) new potatoes, scrubbed
225 g (8 oz) green beans, topped and tailed
half a cucumber, washed and split lengthwise
4 hard-boiled eggs

225 g (8 oz) small tomatoes, peeled and cut in half
225 g (8 oz) beansprouts, washed and drained
60 ml (4 tbs) peanut butter
15 ml (1 tbs) soy sauce
10 ml (1 dsp) each lemon juice and soft brown sugar
1 cup water

Lay the lettucc or cabbage on a large oval serving plate. Boil the potatoes till just cooked, then put in cold water to cool. Cook the beans for 7 minutes untll they are donc but still crunchy. Allow to cool. Scoop out the seeds of the cucumber and cut into wafer-thin half moons. Shell the eggs and cut them into quarters or eighths. Cut the potatoes in half. Arrange rings of tomatoes, egg pieces, potatoes and green beans on top of the lettuce. Sprinkle the cucumber pieces and the beansprouts over the top. Put all the sauce ingredients into a non-stick pan, bring to the boil, and allow to simmer for 5 minutes. The final sauce should have the consistency of single cream; if it needs a little more water, add it when it's boiled. Allow to cool and pour a little over the salad. Serve the rest separately.

SPINACH WITH
SESAME SEED DRESSING

In Japan cooked spinach is eaten cold. It is surprisingly substantial and very appealing to the western palate.

700 g (1½ lb) fresh leaf spinach, washed
and trimmed
60 ml (4 tbs) sesame paste (tahini)
10 ml (1 dsp) sesame oil

juice of half a lemon
10 ml (1 dsp) soy sauce
5 ml (1 tsp) salt

Bring the spinach leaves to the boil in a saucepan full of water and boil for 3 minutes. Drain thoroughly in a colander and chop up roughly with a knife, while still in the colander, to allow any excess liquid to drain off. You should end up with a block of spinach about the size of a saucer and about 1–2 cm (½–¾ in) thick. Allow it to cool and shape it into an oblong about the length of two large matchboxes. These oblongs can be divided up into 4 portions, similar in shape but smaller in size, one for each diner. Mix together in a bowl the sesame paste, sesame oil, lemon juice, soy sauce and salt to make a sauce. If the tahini is particularly thick you may find that heating it in a saucepan with a tablespoon or two of water will help blend the materials together better; if you do this, allow it to cool before spooning a tablespoon of sauce onto each of the portions of spinach. You can cook the spinach up to 12 hours before and keep it in the fridge. Sauce it only half an hour before eating, otherwise it loses its attractive appearance and the contrast between the pale sauce and the dark green spinach.

ACCOMPANIMENTS

Though I call them accompaniments in the title of this chapter, in fact the foods made from the three great grains – rice, wheat and maize – are the very basis of our exotic cuisines. Rice is cooked in its myriad forms all over Asia; wheat is made into parathas, pittas, breads and noodles from India to China. Maize is made into tortillas, tamales and tacos across South America. From puris to pilaus to pancakes, the variety and choice of staples to accompany exotic dishes is huge. As so often with foods, natural marriages exist: tandoori-cooked meats and naan, steamed pancakes and spiced duck, rice and peas with chicken fricassée.

The three grains, in their various guises, have spread all across the world and are now eaten universally. But even in the lands of their origin there are surprises. China, where rice has been cultivated for more than 5,000 years, is only partly a rice-eating nation. In the north, where the weather is wrong for rice but right for wheat, noodles and steamed buns have always been the basic staple, with rice a luxury. The same is true in the north of India where the famous breads, chapatis, puris and parathas are first-choice accompaniments and rice, when it appears, is a special dish, often served on its own. There are also far more varieties of most grains than we might expect. In a wholefood store near where I live there are nine different kinds of rice on sale and that is by no means an exhaustive selection. I've tried to stick to the main varieties of all the grains and to explain what you can do with them. The secret is to understand why the different varieties have been cultivated and the ways in which they complement different sorts of dishes.

Exotic ingredients

Rice

I suggest four different ways of cooking rice as a basic accompaniment, and a couple of more elaborate dishes to go with certain types of cuisine or food. The four basic methods are: the basic Indian method; the rather fancy but scrumptious Persian method using very long grain rice; the Japanese method; and the slightly different Chinese method of rice cooking. Each requires a certain kind of rice and a slightly different approach, but each suits the particular country's style of cooking, down to the way that the food is eaten. Chinese rice, for example, is slightly less sticky than Japanese rice which is eaten with much slenderer chopsticks that have a lot less grip and therefore need the stickiness.

INDIAN STYLE RICE

This is made with long grain rice, sometimes sold as Patna, or you can use Basmati, which is the most expensive long grain rice, with a superb flavour of its own. The method is very simple and produces rice that is thoroughly cooked but free running when it's finished. It is meant to complement the drier and richer curries of northern and central India.

All recipes are for four

225 g (8 oz) long grain rice
5 ml (1 tsp) salt

15 ml (1 tbs) oil
2 litres (4 pints) fresh cold water

Put the rice in a sieve or colander and run cold water through it repeatedly for about a minute, shaking the colander, so that the starch is washed off the rice and the water runs, by the end, very nearly clear. You can also do this by putting the rice in a bowl, pouring the water in, and draining it out through the colander two or three times. Put the rice into a large saucepan, add the salt and oil, and cover with the measured quantity of water. Bring to the boil, then turn down the heat to leave to boil, uncovered, for 8–10 minutes. At this point test a couple of grains of rice: they should be cooked through, with no central bite but still firm. Drain the rice and pour through half a saucepan of hot or boiling water to wash off any residual starch. Pile into a serving dish and allow to stand for 2–3 minutes before serving.

PERSIAN STYLE RICE

The Iranians have long held the reputation for being the greatest rice cookers in the world, though there are Chinese people who might dispute this. Certainly, where long grain rice cooking is concerned, they are outstanding and this method, though it is a little more complicated than the others, produces a dish that for flavour and texture is difficult to beat. This rice tastes so good that it can almost be eaten on its own, as it sometimes is when made from the special black-tipped super-long grain rice that's only available in Iran. The rice to use in this country is Basmati which, though expensive, has both the elegance and flavour that this excellent dish requires.

350 g (12 oz) Basmati rice
15 ml + 5 ml (1 tbs + 1 tsp) salt

30 ml (2 tbs) clarified butter
2.75 litres (5 pints) cold water

Wash the rice in a sieve or colander in plenty of cold water for 1 minute until the water runs clear. Place in a bowl and cover with hot water, adding the tablespoon of salt. Leave for 30 minutes (you can leave it for up to 1½ hours). Drain and place in a clean saucepan with the measured cold water and the teaspoon of salt. Bring to the boil and simmer for 7 minutes. Drain again: you will find the rice almost cooked and the grains greatly expanded in size. In the same saucepan, melt the butter until it stops sizzling, pour in the rice and shake it to make an even layer on the bottom. Cover the saucepan with a clean tea towel and put the lid on. Put it over the lowest possible heat, using an asbestos mat if you've got one, and leave for 15–25 minutes. The rice continues to steam over the heat and the bottom layer, in contact with the butter, forms a crisp coating known as 'dig'. To serve, pour the free-flowing steamed rice into a bowl and scrape the 'dig' off the bottom of the pan with a spatula. It should break up into pieces about the size of a postage stamp and be crispy and golden brown in colour. It will have a wonderful nutty flavour and it is normally sprinkled over the free-flowing rice before it is served.

Pilau rice, rice and peas, Persian style rice

JAPANESE RICE

Japanese rice is always eaten at the end of a meal; only occasionally does it accompany dishes, although it is sometimes eaten in its own right, with flavourings pressed into or poured over it. Rice is the core of all Japanese food, indeed, in Japanese the phrase having a meal is known as 'having your rice'. The Samurai, the warrior caste of Japan, used to be paid in quantities of rice as their annual wages. Their basic method of cooking rice is extremely easy, whether you're going to present it simply in a bowl or as a sushi or donburi, of which more in a moment. The Japanese have taken to electric steamers in a big way for cooking rice as the steamers always produce perfectly cooked rice and can be left unattended. If you have a rice steamer, great, but if not, the method below produces very satisfactory Japanese style rice. The actual grain you need is halfway between long and short grain rice. The short grain rice that we have in Britain is specifically designed to melt away for the purposes of puddings and is therefore not suitable. Most wholefood stores sell Japanese style rice. If you can't find it, buy one of the shorter, long grain types of rice that come from America, if you'll pardon the Irishness of the suggestion for a Japanese dish.

350 g (12 oz) rice
350 ml (¾ pint) water

5 ml (1 tsp) salt

Put the rice into a big bowl and add about a litre (two pints) of cold water. Stir about with chopsticks (or your fingers) until the starch comes off the rice into the water. Drain carefully and place the rice in a saucepan. Add the measured quantity of water and the salt. Bring to the boil and turn down immediately to the lowest possible heat. Cook for 6–8 minutes. When all the visible water has been absorbed, turn the heat off, cover the rice with a piece of kitchen paper under the lid and leave to stand for 10–15 minutes. Tip the rice into a bowl to serve it, breaking it up a little with chopsticks. You will find that it is quite sticky and tends to form small clumps, ideal for eating with thin, Japanese-style chopsticks. The rice is often eaten at the end of a meal with a few salted pickles (see page 227) to flavour it; it is not used to soak up sauces in the way that Chinese style rice is.

Javanese rice cone

Indian and Other Breads

There are two main categories of Indian bread. They are all basically flat by our standards but some are baked on a griddle and some are oven-baked (often in a tandoori oven, which is a great clay pot buried three-quarters in the earth with a charcoal fire lit inside it to heat the air and walls). All Indian breads are used not only to accompany food but as a means of actually eating it, a piece being torn off and held in the right hand to pick up or scoop up meat, vegetables and pulses. These Indian breads tend to be eaten mainly in the north of India, where wheat is the main crop rather than rice.

The three breads I have suggested vary in richness. The simplest, chapatis, are virtually fat-free, parathas are layered with clarified Indian butter, and puris are actually cooked in ghee or butter and are the richest of all. The flour used for this kind of bread baking is called *attar*, it's a fine-milled wholemeal flour and can be found in any Indian grocers or wholefood specialists. If you can't find this actual flour, a mixture of strong white bread flour and fine-ground English wholemeal bread flour will make an adequate substitute. Although flat, all these breads are fairly filling so the average amount is one or at most two of the smaller ones per person. All the recipes are designed to feed four.

CHAPATIS

These are the simplest of all Indian breads and are cooked very quickly on a hot griddle or in a heavy flat-bottomed frying pan, either non-stick or well seasoned; both work very satisfactorily.

225 g (8 oz) attar flour, or a mixture of wholemeal and white bread flours
2.5 ml (½ tsp) salt

125 ml (¼ pint) warm water
5 ml (1 tsp) oil to grease the pan or griddle

Sift the flours together with the salt and mix in the water, using a spoon or your hands. The dough will be sticky at first but should dry out to a firm, pliable mixture after a moment or two. Knead it well. If it is too dry, add a drop more water; if it is too wet, sprinkle a little more flour over it. It should become quite firm and elastic after 2 minutes kneading (you can do this in a food processor, for about 15 seconds). Put the dough to stand (not in the fridge) for 15–20 minutes. Divide into 8 balls and, on a floured board with a floured rolling pin, roll the balls out as flat as you can. They should spread to the size of a small dinner or large tea plate.

Grease the griddle or frying pan very lightly and heat until hot. Put a chapati on the surface, press down with your fingers or a fish slice, and move after about 30 seconds. After a minute turn it over: it should be pale brown with a few darker brown spots on it. Press down on the other side and cook for another 30–60 seconds. Take off the heat, put on a warm plate and cover with a damp tea towel. Repeat until all the chapatis are made; the towel stops them drying out as they wait to be eaten.

PARATHAS

This is a form of Indian bread that's rather richer than the simple chapati. It has melted clarified butter spread between the layers of dough before it's cooked, giving it a very flaky and melt-in-the-mouth effect.

350 g (12 oz) attar flour, or a mixture of strong white and fine-ground wholemeal bread flours

100 g (4 oz) ghee or butter
2.5 ml (½ tsp) salt
15 ml (1 tbs) oil

Rub 1 tablespoon of the clarified butter or fresh butter into the flour with your fingers to make coarse breadcrumbs. Add the salt and 8 tablespoons of cold water. This should make a firm but pliable dough. If it is too dry add a little more water, since different flours absorb water at different levels. If it is too damp, sprinkle a little more white bread flour over it. Knead the mixture for 2 minutes and divide into 8 portions. Roll each portion out into a rough oval and spread like toast with some of the ghee or butter. Fold in half, spread again, fold over and spread again, folding each paratha three times in all. (As you cook one paratha you can carry out this process with each successive paratha.) Roll out into either a round shape or, if you find this too difficult to achieve, into the triangular shape that the folding has left with you. Although most parathas are made round, there is a strong tradition of triangular shaped ones, especially when eating food in the open air. Heat the griddle or frying pan, smear with a little oil, and cook each paratha for 2 minutes each side, pressing down with your fingers or a fish slice to make sure that the whole surface makes contact with the griddle. These can be stored as you make them in a slightly damp tea towel and reheated in the oven wrapped in foil if necessary.

PURIS

These are the richest of all forms of Indian bread and are normally served as a basis for a rich curry served in a small pile on top of them, or as a means of eating a small quantity of quite simply cooked food which contrasts with the richness of the puris themselves. They can also be used to accompany sweet things.

225 g (8 oz) attar flour or equal quantities of white bread flour and fine-ground wholemeal flour
30 ml (2 tbs) ghee or melted butter

2.5 ml (½ tsp) salt
125 ml (¼ pint) oil (or melted ghee) for cooking

Rub the butter or ghee into the flour and add the salt. Add 5 tablespoons of cold water, one at a time, and mix to a soft dough. Knead for 2 minutes and put aside. Put the cooking oil or melted ghee into a small frying pan, not more than 18 cm (7 in) across, so that it forms a depth of about 5 mm (¼ in), and heat it till it's as hot as you can get it before it smokes. Divide the dough into 8 pieces and roll out each one in succession, as you cook the puri before it, into a circle approximately the size of a saucer. Place the puri in the hot oil, being very careful not to drop it but to slide it in. Press down with a fish slice or similar tool and you will find that the puri will spring and puff up, rather like a cushion. Turn it over quickly and cook the other side. The whole cooking process should not take more than 1–1½ minutes. If the puri fails to inflate, it will still taste delicious though it won't look as good. These are best eaten as soon as they are cooked so they are the sort of thing I cook when I've got friends sitting in the kitchen looking hungrily appreciative.

NAANS

This is one of the oven-baked breads of India and is really a leavened bread, though it comes out pretty flat by our standards. It's traditionally cooked in a tandoori oven where it's slapped onto the inside of the huge clay jar so that it sticks while it cooks and you have one flat side and one bubbled side. You can do this perfectly well in a conventional oven on a lightly greased baking tray. Naans are quite filling and I think that half a large one each, to accompany kebabs or dry meat dishes like the Bhuna Ghosht (page 104), is ample. Like chapatis and parathas, they reheat quite well in a foil pack in a medium oven. Originally naans were raised by a combination of the action of yoghurt and fermentation but a little baking powder helps the matter along very well these days.

225 g (8 oz) plain white flour
2.5 ml (½ tsp) baking powder
2.5 ml (½ tsp) salt

100–125 g (4–5 oz) plain low fat yoghurt,
beaten with a fork

Sift the flour into a bowl, add the salt and baking powder and mix. Add the yoghurt and make a soft dough with the flour mixture. It should be quite pliable and shapeable with your hands. Adjust the amounts of flour or yoghurt to achieve this, if necessary. Knead it for a minute and leave it to stand for half an hour in a warm place, covered with a cloth or some clingfilm. Heat your oven to very hot (210°C, 425°F, Gas mark 7) and put in your lightly greased baking tray to heat up. Divide the dough into 4 equal parts and roll out with a rolling pin into long ovals. When your oven is hot enough, slap the 4 naans on to the baking sheet, put back into the oven and keep the heat at the high level. They will cook in about 8–10 minutes, puffing up into bubbles on the top. When they are lightly browned in places on the top, remove them. They should still be pale in patches and completely flexible. You can brush them with melted butter at this stage if you like and eat them quickly while they are still warm. They can also be reheated in aluminium foil.

Chapatis, parathas, peshawari naans, pitta, poppadums

PESHAWARI NAANS

These are a slightly exotic version of the naan, eaten in the area around Peshawar. They have a wonderful fragrant mixture of honey, spices and nuts inserted into the dough and are very reminiscent of the nomadic influences on food from this part of north-west India. This is quite a simple version of the spiced bread. Grand versions are sometimes made on a very large scale, the bread being up to a metre (2–3 feet) across, for special banquets or feasts. The quantity of filling given below will fill 4–6 naans.

1 naan (recipe as above)
25 g (1 oz) pistachio nuts (shelled)
25 g (1 oz) slivered almonds
2.5 ml (½ tsp) each ground cloves and ground cinnamon

25 g (1 oz) large stoneless raisins, roughly chopped
60 ml (4 tbs) thick honey

Make the naan mixture as above up to the point where it is standing and rising. Chop the pistachios and mix with the slivered almonds, then add the spices and chopped raisins. As you roll out each bread, spread it with 2 teaspoonfuls of honey, not quite reaching the edges, then sprinkle with a portion of the spiced nut and fruit mixture. Fold the naan over, pressing the edges down to make sure that the filling is sealed in, then flour and roll out again into the oval shape before baking, as above. The honey, fruit and nut mixture is a wonderful surprise as you eat the bread.

PITTAS

These breads from the Middle East are eaten in varying forms from the Atlantic coast of North Africa right the way across to the eastern edge of Turkey. They are leavened with yeast and come in various shapes and thicknesses. They are also made with a variety of flours and, although wholemeal ones are very popular, I prefer those made with a mixture of flours, with a little wholemeal for texture and white flour for lightness. You can make quite a big batch in advance if you like, by doubling or trebling the quantities, and keeping them when they've cooled in plastic bags in the fridge. They reheat very well. The great trick with pittas is to make sure that they don't cook to anything more than a very pale creamy brown on the first cooking, otherwise they won't remain pliable and separate into the pockets that are so convenient for stuffing with salads and kebabs. They only separate well, by the way, when they're hot (either freshly cooked or reheated), so if you want to fill them make sure they are warm when you cut them open down one side. These make slightly fatter pittas than the ones that are sold commercially and are all the better for it in my opinion.

450 g (1 lb) strong white bread flour
50 g (2 oz) wholemeal bread flour
half a packet of dried instant yeast
2.5 ml (½ tsp) salt

5 ml (1 tsp) sugar
15 ml (1 tbs) olive oil
generous 250 ml (½ pint) water

Sift the flour, dried yeast, salt and sugar together. Stir in the oil without troubling yourself too much about a smooth mixture at this stage. Heat the water to blood heat (hot enough to keep your little finger in it for a count of ten without screaming, but able to feel the heat). Mix the water into the flour and knead thoroughly for 2–3 minutes (this can be done in a food processor for about 30 seconds if you prefer). You should end up with a soft and pliable dough. Put it in a warm place with a cloth over it to rise for 1 hour. You may like to grease the bowl lightly with a little more oil when you do this to prevent it sticking when it rises. At the end of the hour, knead the mixture again, which will cause it to deflate considerably – do not panic. Divide it into 6 portions and roll these out into either ovals or rounds. Put them to rise again on a floured baking sheet or tray for another 30–45 minutes. Cover them with a tea towel. Turn your oven to 220°C, 450°F, Gas mark 8, and preheat 2 baking sheets. When the pittas have risen again, lift them carefully with a fish slice or spatula and place on the baking sheets. Put into the oven and bake for 5–8 minutes, checking them after 5 minutes. They are meant to be pale creamy gold with perhaps a fleck or two of brown but not more, otherwise they will go hard and biscuit-like, which is not the object at all. Remove them carefully and allow to cool a little before eating or storing.

POPPADUMS

These are the crispy mini-breads that are eaten as a texture contrast with a lot of sub-continental foods. No-one, even in India, makes poppadums themselves these days, unless they are an incredible purist. You can buy packets of them, ready to cook, in any Indian grocers and in many wholefood shops and supermarkets. They come in a variety of sizes and flavours. The plain ones, which we are perhaps most familiar with, are about the size of a small dinner plate and are made from gram flour or ground up chick peas. There are also flavoured ones. My favourite are the ones with fresh garlic in, which can be identified not only by name but by the visible tiny green flecks of the appetizing bulb in them. They are smaller in size than the plain ones, about the size of a saucer, and slightly thicker. So too are the spiced ones, the *masala papads* which have black pepper and other spices worked through them. You can occasionally find even more exotic varieties, but those three are the most common.

Poppadums can be cooked in two different ways. Traditionally they were flash fried in hot oil in a *karai*, a kind of mini black-iron wok which had melted ghee or oil in the bottom of it. They took only about 25–30 seconds to cook in this way and a pile of them was normally served in a basket. You can do this in a frying pan equally well. If you're looking for a slightly more healthy approach than this high-fat way of cooking, poppadums grill or oven-bake equally well. The grill or oven needs to be *very* hot and you need to keep a close eye on them but, once again, they only take about 35–60 seconds to cook. You can tell when poppadums are done because they lose their slightly shiny, oiled-looking surface and become rather sandy in texture and appearance when they've been grilled or oven-baked. Serve one or two, possibly of varying flavours, per person to go with an Indian or other spicy meal.

PEKING DUCK PANCAKES

These are the pancakes traditionally used to wrap up Peking Duck with its flavours and fragrances (see page 74), but in north China pancakes like this are eaten with other dishes as well. They are quite simple to make though they do take a little time so if you're pressed you can buy them in Chinese supermarkets or wholefood shops. Make sure you have enough pancakes: I find that the traditional two or three served with Peking Duck are never enough once you have tasted how delicious the duck is. I think six each is a good working basis – but then I am an enthusiast!

450 g (1 lb) plain white flour, sieved
2.5 ml (½ tsp) salt
180 ml (12 tbs) boiling water

60 ml (2 tbs) cold water
60 ml (2 tbs) oil (preferably sesame oil)

Mix the salt and sieved flour together in a basin. Pour the boiling water onto the flour in one go and stir vigorously with a fork (it's too hot to handle at this stage). Add the cold water and, as soon as the dough is cool enough to be handled, knead it thoroughly for a couple of minutes. This can be done in a food processor for 35–40 seconds if you wish. Once it's kneaded leave it to stand in a covered bowl for about 15 minutes. Divide it into half and roll out each half into a cylindrical shape about 30 cm (12 in) long and as even as you can make it. Divide the cylinder into 2.5 cm (1 in) pieces and roll out each of these, using a floured rolling pin and board, into a circle approximately the size of a small saucer. Brush the first pancake with a little of the oil, roll out the second pancake, press it onto the first pancake and set aside. Do the same again until you have used up all the pieces of dough, so you have 12 double pancakes. Heat a griddle or large heavy non-stick frying pan until very hot, and brush lightly with the remaining oil. Place a double pancake, or two if your pan or griddle is big enough, onto the hot surface, press down with a spatula or fish slice, and cook for 1 minute. Turn over and do the same on the other side. The pancakes should still be pale creamy coloured with a few flecks of brown on them. When both sides have reached this stage, remove and peel apart so that you have 24 pancakes with only one side browned. Stack them in a damp tea towel until you have finished all of them. To serve, place the tea towel of pancakes in a steamer and steam for 5 minutes over boiling water. The diners put their duck and fillings on the uncooked side of the pancake, roll up and eat as described on page 74.

Noodles

Pasta in general is a source of great dispute. The Italians claim that it was being eaten in some form in Roman days, the Chinese claim to have been eating it for at least 3,000 years, and the general wisdom is that our broadscale knowledge of pasta was brought by Marco Polo back to Venice after his visits to the Great Khan in the fourteenth century. It then spread through Italy and in due course the rest of the western world. Whichever origin you prefer, there is no question that noodles are a universal food (with the surprising exception of the pre-Europeanized cuisine of the American continent).

CHINESE NOODLES

Chinese noodles are made from a variety of basic ingredients: wheat, rice and beans or peas. The latter are used to make the cellophane noodles, which are unique to China. If you have access to a Chinese grocery store, they sell a number of these different styles of noodles fresh. In this condition they need cooking for a very brief period of time indeed, not more than 3 minutes. Sometimes they are egg noodles, recognizable by their bright yellow colour, with a slightly richer taste. Fresh noodles will keep in the fridge for two or three days.

Wheat noodles are all flat, rather like Italian *tagliatelle*, but come in three different sizes. The very fine kind that is plaited together in the dried form needs only 3–4 minutes cooking in boiling water. It can also be cooked in very hot oil in a chip pan to produce the nest of noodles that sometimes tops dishes like Chow Mein. To do this, have the oil at cooking temperature and, to a normal-sized chip pan, add 225 g (8 oz) fine wheat noodles in their original plaits. They will expand, almost explode (not dangerously), to fill the available space as they come into contact with the hot oil and should be lifted out after about a minute, when they will be golden brown and very crunchy.

The next size of noodles is approximately the same as Italian *tagliatelle* in thickness, though once again they will cook faster than European pasta. They should be cooked for approximately 5 minutes in boiling water. In Shanghai they produce an even bigger noodle, nearly 2.5 cm (1 in) across, and sometimes even larger. These are used for Shanghai-style stir fry dishes and are not eaten in most other parts of China. If you can obtain them from a Chinese shop, they need cooking for about 7–8 minutes and are very good with the beef dish on page 99.

Rice noodles, like wheat noodles, come in a series of sizes. The finest are like hair and are normally only used in soups. Medium-thickness rice noodles and thick noodles, which are sometimes obtainable in this country, are almost always rounded. They can be cooked like the wheat noodles in boiling water for 3 or 4 minutes but are often presoaked instead for up to 10–15 minutes in water that has been boiling, and are then stir-fried or cooked in sauces which they will absorb.

Cellophane noodles or bean starch noodles are very different. They are almost transparent, as their name suggests, and are used almost exclusively to absorb and carry sauces. If you have made a Chinese dish (like Kungpao Chicken, page 66) with a lot of sauce left over, or if you wish to expand the dish to serve more people, or the sauce is just too intense on its own, soak 50–75 g (2–3 oz) of these cellophane noodles in hot water for about 5 minutes before adding them to the dish. They add no flavour of their own but give quite a savoury texture and carry the flavours of the sauces remarkably well.

JAPANESE NOODLES

The Japanese have a variety of noodle ingredients. They have rice noodles of a very similar sort to the Chinese, though they generally prefer wheat noodles and buckwheat noodles. These last tend to come in two sizes, thin and thick. They are called *soba* and are very solid and substantial to eat. They have a slightly wholewheat appearance and are used, particularly the thicker kind, in dishes with many other ingredients, like Sukiyaki on page 100. They also have two thicknesses of wheat noodles, *somen* and *udon*, the latter thicker ones being used in the noodle-dishes that are a part of Japanese fast-food culture.

OTHER NOODLES

There are other kinds of pasta and noodles to be found all over India and the Middle East under various names like *sev* or *rishta*. They are made from a variety of ingredients like gram flour, rice and wheat, and they are eaten in an incredible variety of ways. They may be deep fried in small sections, as you will find in what is known in this country as Bombay Mix, through to baked dishes almost Italian in style and flavour in the high mountains of the Caucasus and the Hindu Kush. They are almost all impossible to buy in their original form in this country.

Pineapple shell salad

MATRIMONY

This is a West Indian combination of oranges and freshly grated coconut, thought to be so perfect that it earned the title of Matrimony! The ingredients are not difficult to find if you remember that all the coconuts at which we throw balls at fairs can be opened and have their crisp white flesh grated. Serve this in a big glass bowl in the middle of the table, after chilling it in the fridge for at least an hour or two before your eat it. The hour also allows the flavours to marry.

4 large or 6 medium oranges
25 g (1 oz) caster sugar

1.25 ml (¼ tsp) allspice
100 g (4 oz) fresh coconut

Peel the oranges, removing as much as you can of the white pith, and slice across the grain into rounds 5 mm (¼ in) thick. Remove any seeds or pips and put the slices in overlapping rings in the bottom of a large and attractive glass bowl. Mix the sugar and the allspice and sprinkle that over the top. Peel any brown skin off the chunks of coconut and grate it either in a hand grater of in a food processor. Sprinkle the freshly grated coconut over the top of the orange segments and tilt the bowl gently to pick up some of the juice that will be running out of the oranges. Spoon that in turn over the coconut until all of it has been doused. Cover with clingfilm and refrigerate for 1–2 hours before serving.

KUMQUATS IN GINGER

This is a Chinese-style fruit salad which is made with the tiny bitter-sweet oranges grown in China and South East Asia that can be eaten whole.

450 g (1 lb) kumquats
250 ml (½ pint) water

100 g (4 oz) granulated sugar
100 g (4 oz) preserved ginger in syrup

PASSION FRUIT SHERBET

Passion fruit, also known as granadillas, are extremely common all over the Tropics, and come in different sizes and shapes. It is possible to buy passion fruit juice as well, and that makes a very good version of this sorbet, which is tart and delicious. But do try to include one or two fresh passion fruit as the little black pips in it are often included in the sorbet as evidence of its fruit origins. If you're making the ice cream from scratch with fresh passion fruit, you do need quite a lot. So if you care to mix the juice with orange juice and make an orange and passion fruit sorbet, that's fine and will still taste delicious.

100 g (4 oz) caster sugar
125 ml (5 fl oz) water
2 egg whites

250 ml (½ pint) passion fruit juice from the pulp scooped from 10–12 passion fruit, or a carton of passion fruit juice plus 2 passion fruit

Make a syrup with the sugar and water, boiling it hard until a drop on a cold saucer forms a rubbery blob, rather like testing for setting jam. Allow it to cool and mix in the passion fruit pulp or juice. Pour it into a container and put in the freezer or into an ice cream maker. Freeze for 2 hours, take out, and whisk or process in a food processor until the mixture is as smooth as possible; it will be like slush at this point. Beat the egg whites until they are firm, then fold in, and refreeze for another 2 hours. If using an ice cream maker, freeze until the mixture is semi-solid, add the beaten egg whites, and finish freezing. Allow to set for at least 4 hours after adding the egg whites. To serve, let the ice cream sit in the fridge for at least half an hour before scooping into wine glasses in attractive shaped balls.

Ginger ice cream, lychee sorbet, passion fruit and orange sorbet

TROPICAL TIRAMISU

One of the most popular puddings in Europe in recent years has been Tiramisu, an Italian cream cheese pudding of amazing flavour and formidable calories. Here is a tropical or exotic equivalent using the flavours of coconut rather than dairy products as their basis. Like Tiramisu however it's very rich and not a slimming recipe so it should be eaten in moderate quantities.

---

375 g (12 oz) sweet coconut biscuits (not cream biscuits)
1 cup of strong black coffee
375 g 2 (12 oz) tins coconut cream

100 g (4 oz) grated dark chocolate
2.5 ml (¹/₂ tsp) cinnamon

Soak the coconut biscuits in the cup of coffee, mashing them up with a fork so that they break into bits. Open the tins of coconut milk, which you will find contain a thick creamy mixture and some quite runny liquid. Spoon out the cream and put it into a bowl. You can use the liquid for cooking some of the other dishes in the book as coconut milk, but you only want the cream for this recipe. Stir in the cinnamon and mix thoroughly until it's smooth. Into a bowl in which all the mixture will fit, put a layer of a third of the biscuits. Add half the coconut cream, another layer of biscuits, spread over half the chocolate, another layer of cream, the last of the biscuits and the last layer of chocolate. Tap the bowl gently to make sure that it's settled and all the air that might have been trapped is out, and chill the pudding for at least 2 hours. It is possible to make this in individual pots but make sure that you don't overdo the portions.

FLAN

This is a Mexican dish, indeed it's almost the national dessert of Mexico, but clearly is not indigenous in the sense that it was there before Columbus arrived. It is supposed to have gained its popularity from a dish made by Catholic nuns who were running a mission in the country. It is a delicious form of creme caramel or egg custard, and the slight spicing of cinnamon, which is very Mexican, adds an unexpected note of grace.

250 ml (½ pint) milk
50 g (2 oz) caster sugar
2.5 ml (½ tsp) cinnamon

2 eggs + 1 yolk
50 g (2 oz) granulated sugar
30 ml (2 tbs) water

Put the milk into a saucepan with the caster sugar, bring to the boil and simmer for 2–3 minutes. Add the cinnamon and stir, then leave to cool. Beat the eggs and egg yolk until they are lemon coloured and strain through a sieve into the milk mixture. Whisk quickly and leave to stand aside while you bring the granulated sugar and water to a boil in a non-stick pan. Allow it to caramelize, that is go medium brown and smell like toffee – do not let it burn and be careful about it spitting. In a small 500 ml (1 pint) soufflé dish, pour in the caramel and allow it to partially set – this will take about 5 minutes. Pour the egg and milk mixture in. Put the soufflé dish into a baking tin into which you have poured about 800 ml (1½ pints) of hot water. Place in a medium oven (180°C, 350°F, Gas Mark 4), and bake for 35–40 minutes until the custard is set. Allow to cool before turning out. The easiest way to turn it out is to immerse the bottom of the soufflé dish into a little hot water for about 10–20 seconds, slide a knife around the edge of the custard, place a plate upside down on top of the soufflé dish and turn the whole lot over with one quick motion. The caramel custard should slide out onto the plate and be served from there. You will have a pleasant combination of creamy custard and rich sauce.

COFFEE BRIGADEIROS

Unusual ingredients are often part of exotic cooking and few are more unusual than condensed milk but it's surprisingly widely used, not only in South America but also in Africa. Because of the temperature and before widespread refrigeration was available, it was often the only way that milk could be kept. This recipe does also, however, make use of the most famous Brazilian ingredient which is coffee to make what is essentially a sweetmeat to be eaten with a cup of coffee as a closing to a meal.

1 can sweetened condensed milk
15 ml (1 tbs) cocoa
⅓ cup strong coffee

15 ml (1 tbs) butter
½ cup grated coconut

Put all the ingredients except the coconut into a non-stick saucepan. Cook over a low heat until everything has melted and the mixture is smooth. Pour into a greased bowl and allow to cool. When it is cold, wet your hands and shape the mixture into little balls which you then roll in the grated coconut. Chill for 1 hour before serving.

Coffee brigadeiros

BUDIN DE PAN (Bread Pudding)

As the name of this dish will tell you, it's not an Argentinian original. In fact it's as much eaten in Uruguay as it is in Argentina and clearly was imported by the many European immigrants who make up the bulk of the population. It's a slight twist on our own bread pudding but none the worse for that. It's eaten however as a pudding, not as a cake, and if you don't fancy ice-cream with it as I suggest, it goes very well with fromage frais whose slight edge cuts the sweetness.

225 g (8 oz) fresh breadcrumbs
250 ml (½ pint) milk
45 ml (3 tbs) sugar
3 eggs

pinch of salt
grated lemon rind – preferably unwaxed
100 g (4 oz) granulated sugar
handful of seedless raisins

Put the breadcrumbs into a large bowl. Bring the milk to the boil, pour over the breadcrumbs and leave them to soak. In another bowl, beat the eggs, 3 tablespoons of the sugar and the pinch of salt. You want this to be well blended rather than foamy. Pour this over the breadcrumbs and milk and add the grated lemon rind and the raisins. Mix well. Pour the granulated sugar into a heavy based saucepan and melt it over a medium heat until the sugar turns to liquid and goes golden. Take it off the heat at once. Pour it very carefully into a greased and warmed bread tin or ovenproof dish and carefully but quickly tip the warmed dish so it is lined with the caramel. You need to be quick as the caramel solidifies very rapidly. Wear oven gloves as the caramel is burning hot. Pour the bread mixture into the dish, smooth the top and bake it in a low oven, 325°F/160°C/150°C Fan/Gas mark 3/bottom of the Aga, for about 45 minutes to an hour. Wait until it is completely cold before turning out. Serve with very good vanilla ice-cream.

Budin de pan (top); Matrimony (bottom)

SNACKS, STREET FOOD AND RELISHES

Fast food has a long history. We may think that our hamburger palaces and pizza joints, our fish and chip and doner kebab shops are a new development, but street food – snacks to be eaten not at a formal meal but when the need or the appetite takes you – are as old as streets themselves. Almost all the traditional cuisines have street food in some form or another. And this is especially so in the tropical countries where life is lived more out of doors than in, where street markets abound, and where it was difficult to store food before the advent of refrigeration. All across the Indian sub-continent you find street snacks such as kebabs and samosas, chapatis and parathas stuffed with vegetables and meat, banana-leaf cups containing crisp, crunchy or soft and spicy fillings, sweet-meats, and refreshing drinks. In Indonesia, there are satés and mutabak, thin pastries filled with spiced meats and vegetables. North Africa has 'bricks', paper-thin, flash-fried pastries a foot wide containing fish and vegetables, sauced with an egg still soft inside them. In Turkey and the eastern Mediterranean, there is bread, particularly pitta bread, filled with spiced bean patés, aubergine dips, thinly sliced crisp roast lamb, salads and chutneys. In Mexico, the markets sell cornmeal tortillas, crisply fried and holding spiced beef, salads and cheeses. In Argentina, pastries are filled with meat and peaches and pears, and in Japan yakitori, tiny skewers of chicken are dipped in soy sauce and grilled to a shiny glaze. Street food, fast food, abounds everywhere, full of delicious flavours and instant pleasures.

In some parts of the world this kind of eating has been brought to a very sophisticated level. In South East Asia the hawker markets and night bazaars often contain up to a hundred stalls, each specializing in a different dish. One may do kebabs, another a fish soup, a third a rice dish, a fourth grilled squid, a fifth two or three special curries, and so on. In order to eat from these stalls you wander about looking at all the alternative dishes, choose your meal and order each dish from the appropriate stall. You then find one of the tables usually set off to one side under the trees, or by the beach, or in the town square, give the table number to your stalls, and they will deliver the food to you to be paid for as it arrives. It's a great way to eat, usually very cheap, always great fun,

SAMOSAS

I'm giving two recipes for samosas. The pastry is the same for both of them but one filling is vegetarian and the other is meat. Samosas are very easy to make and can be prepared in advance and stored in the fridge to be deep fried when you're ready. Since some people prefer samosas to be baked in the oven to reduce the fat content (even though it doesn't give quite such a crisp finish as the old-fashioned oil method), I've given both sets of instructions below. Samosas are traditionally eaten with a herb chutney, mint and cucumber, sometimes with yoghurt, always with the fingers.

Pastry

200 g (8 oz) plain white flour
pinch of salt

100 g (4 oz) butter or soft margarine

You can make this by hand, rubbing the margarine, salt and flour together with your fingertips and then adding 3–4 tablespoons of water very slowly until you get a soft dough. I always use a food processor because it's easier, quicker and, frankly, makes better dough than I can by hand. Put all the ingredients, except the water, into the food processor and process for a few seconds until the mixture resembles fine breadcrumbs. Gradually add 3–4 tablespoons of water while the machine is running until the dough forms a soft ball. Chill the pastry, wrapped in a piece of greaseproof paper, in the fridge for about 30 minutes. Let it warm up a little before dividing it into 8 pieces. Roll each piece into a ball.

Vegetarian Filling

60 ml (4 tbs) ghee (see Ingredients, page 6)
or cooking oil
1 onion, peeled and finely chopped
5 ml (1 tsp) each turmeric, ground cumin
and ground coriander

2.5 ml (½ tsp) each ground ginger, salt and
chilli powder
450 g (1 lb) potatoes, peeled and chopped
into very small dice
150 g (6 oz) frozen peas
fresh coriander or parsley, chopped

Put the oil or ghee into a pan, add the onion and the spices and fry gently together for 3 minutes. Add the potatoes and just enough water to cover, bring to the boil and simmer for 5 minutes. Add the peas and cook for another minute. Stir in the chopped coriander or parsley and allow the mixture to cool. Roll out the balls of dough on a floured surface until about 15–18 cm (6–7 in) in diameter. Cut each one in half with a sharp knife and make each half circle into a cone, sealing the edges by moistening them with water or egg white. Put a generous tablespoon of filling into each cone, being careful not to overfill them, and crimp the top of the cone together again using water or egg white to seal. Put aside until you have made all 16 samosas. Heat either your deep fryer or 2.5 cm (1 in) of oil in a generous sized pan and fry the samosas to a golden colour on each side – this will take approximately 3–4 minutes in the shallow oil on each side, 2–3 minutes in the deep frying oil. Or bake the samosas on a greased tray in a hot oven (190°C, 375°F, Gas mark 5) for 10–12 minutes until golden.

Meat Filling

1 large onion, peeled and finely chopped
1 clove garlic, peeled and finely chopped
5 ml (1 tsp) each ground cumin, ground coriander and garam masala
2.5 ml (½ tsp) each black pepper and ground ginger

1 pinch each ground cloves and cinnamon
15 ml (1 tbs) ghee or frying oil
225 g (8 oz) ground lamb or beef
salt

Fry the onion and garlic together with the spices in the ghee or oil for 2–3 minutes until softened. Add the meat and brown carefully for 4–5 minutes. Add 4 tablespoons of water to moisten the mixture, add salt to taste and cook for another 5 minutes, then allow to cool. Roll out the pastry as above into circles, cut in half and fill each with the meat mixture, making sure that the pastry edges are carefully sealed. Fry as for the vegetable samosas in a deep fryer or in shallow oil in a generous saucepan.

A selection of street food

ONION BHAJI

In my family this is known as 'the easiest thing in the world' from an ill-advised casual remark I once made while in the process of cooking some. In fact, made in the way I make them, onion bhajis *are* terribly easy since they can be shallow fried and don't have to be moulded into a round shape. They come out rather like little Scotch pancakes but are full of onions and totally delicious. You can make them with a variety of flours but the proper material is gram flour, made from chick peas, which gives a lovely thick, flavourful pancake which complements the onions perfectly. But if you can't find gram flour, then strong white bread flour or plain flour made from wheat is an acceptable substitute. Although they can form part of a larger Indian meal or be eaten as a first course, onion bhajis make a super snack, especially when served with a bowl of yoghurt and some Prawn Balichow, a kind of fish-based pickle that's available on almost all supermarket condiment shelves.

1 egg
225 g (8 oz) gram flour
450 g (1 lb) onions, peeled and sliced into
5 mm (¼ in) rings or half-rings

2.5 ml (½ tsp) salt
15 ml (1 tbs) chopped fresh coriander
(optional)
oil for frying

Beat the egg and add it to the flour, then add the salt and whisk in enough water to make a consistency like double cream. This may seem quite difficult to achieve at first but the mixture will suddenly go smooth. Allow to stand for 15 minutes. Add the onions to the batter and the coriander if used and allow to stand for another 5 minutes as the onions will give off some liquid. Stir thoroughly. Heat a large frying pan, either non-stick or seasoned iron, until it is really hot, then smear with oil and put tablespoons of the onion mixture into it, spaced a little apart; you can put 4 or 5 at once in a 30 cm (12 in) pan. Press down with the back of a spoon and allow to set for 2–3 minutes before turning, pressing down again with a fish slice or spatula. They should be cooked after 1–2 minutes on the second side. Keep them warm until you finish cooking the whole bowlful, which should make about 16 mini pancakes.

LAMB SATÉ

Satés, small pieces of meat on a skewer, quick-grilled and served with a peanut sauce, are one of the great dishes of the world. They originated in Indonesia but rapidly spread through the rest of South East Asia and now appear in restaurants the world over. The basic concept is simple: tiny pieces of meat are marinated in spices, grilled quickly and eaten with a sauce made of roasted ground peanuts with the marinade stirred into it. In its home base of Indonesia, saté was almost always lamb (or mutton) or chicken, but now there are prawn satés, as well as vegetarian satés: all sorts of meat and other ingredients find their way onto the thin bamboo skewers. I think that the closer you get to the traditional origins of the dish, the better the flavours and the more interesting the eating. Don't be tempted to turn any of the satés into kebabs by cutting the meat into larger portions; saté is meant to be served as lots of little skewers, rather than one or two big ones per portion.

450 g (1 lb) boned leg of lamb, cut into pieces the size of a large postage stamp and about 5 mm (¼ in) thick
100 g (4 oz) crunchy peanut butter
15 ml (1 tbs) creamed coconut (block)
1 clove garlic, peeled and finely chopped

60 ml (4 tbs) soy sauce
30 ml (2 tbs) brown sugar
15 ml (1 tbs) lemon juice
5 ml (1 tsp) prawn or anchovy paste
15 ml (1 tbs) chilli sauce
225 ml (8 fl oz) water

Marinate the cubes of meat in the soy sauce, sugar and lemon juice for 2–8 hours. Thread them flat side up onto bamboo skewers (available in any Chinese or Asian shop or supermarket). Mix the remaining ingredients together in a non-stick saucepan. Bring to the boil and stir gently. Although it looks extremely unprepossessing at first, this sauce will thicken and go smooth as it comes to the boil. Add the marinade liquid and simmer for 5 minutes. The sauce should be a dark glossy chocolate-brown. Heat your grill to maximum for 5 minutes and grill the skewers of meat for approximately 2 minutes a side. The meat should be cooked but not shrivelled. To serve, lay the skewers of meat on the shredded lettuce surrounded by the chunks of cucumber, and serve with a little sauce dribbled over them and more in a separate bowl on the side to dip into.

CHICKEN SATÉ

This is probably the favourite saté of all. Serve it with cucumber chunks and rice cakes. These are made from allowing rice cooked in the Chinese manner (page 166) to go cold in the pan and then to cut it up into oblongs about 2.5 cm (1 in) long by 1 cm (½ in) wide. These are dipped in the sauce and eaten with the saté.

---

450 g (1 lb) boneless chicken, cut across the grain into pieces the size of a large postage stamp and about 5 mm (¼ in) thick
1 small onion, peeled and finely chopped
2 cloves garlic, peeled and finely chopped

60 ml (4 tbs) lemon juice
2.5 cm (1 in) piece fresh root ginger, peeled and chopped
2.5 ml (½ tsp) turmeric
60 ml (4 tbs) soy sauce

Sauce

150 g (6 oz) peanuts
15 ml (1 tbs) each brown sugar and chilli sauce (the thick South East Asian kind, not Tabasco)

the marinade
1 cup water

Mix together all the ingredients except the chicken and the sauce materials, then allow the chicken pieces to marinate for at least 2 hours and up to 12 hours. Thread onto thin bamboo skewers lengthwise, so the maximum amount of chicken is exposed to the grill. Preheat the grill for 5 minutes and grill the skewers of chicken for 3–4 minutes each side. The chicken should be cooked but not dry. Meanwhile grind the peanuts – which should be ready roasted or, if raw, browned in a frying pan for 2–3 minutes – in a food processor or liquidizer. You may need to add a little liquid from the marinade to help the blades work. Put the resulting medium to fine mixture into a saucepan, add the rest of the marinade, the other flavouring ingredients, and the cup of water. Bring to the boil and simmer for 10 minutes before serving with the chicken and rice cakes.

JAMAICAN PATTIES

These are Jamaica's answer to the Cornish pasty, and in fact one of the three counties of Jamaica is called Cornwall, but there the resemblance ends. A good pattie is bright gold in colour and is filled with spiced meat and herbs, without a turnip to be seen. Many years ago there was a bakery in Kingston, the capital town of Jamaica, that made patties using a yeast dough that rose at the same time as it baked. They produced patties of such incredible size that they were known locally as elephant burgers, and if you could finish a whole one your reputation amongst the local people soared.

Pastry Ingredients

225 g (8 oz) plain flour
5 ml (1 tsp) turmeric
2.5 ml (½ tsp) salt

75 g (3 oz) margarine or white pastry-
making fat
60 ml (4 tbs) cold water

Sieve together the flour, turmeric and salt, work in the margarine or shortening until the mixture resembles breadcrumbs, then add the water gradually until a firm dough is made. You can do this all in a food processor if you prefer. Allow the dough to rest for at least 30 minutes, though overnight is traditional. Divide it into 8 portions and roll each one out into a saucer-sized piece of pastry. Meanwhile, make the filling.

Filling Ingredients

225 g (8 oz) minced beef
15 ml (1 tbs) cooking oil
1 onion, peeled and finely chopped
2 spring onions, trimmed and finely
chopped

1 small chilli pepper, finely chopped
1 slice bread turned into breadcrumbs
2.5 ml (½ tsp) dried thyme
10 ml (1 dsp) curry powder
salt and pepper

Fry the beef in the oil until well browned, add the onions, chilli and breadcrumbs, thyme and curry powder, and fry again gently for another 5 minutes. Add a cup of and allow to cook 10 minutes until most has evaporated but the still cool a little and divide into filling one circle of dough. moistening and crimping the edges with make sure the pattie bake them at 200°C, 400°F, Gas Mark 6, for about until they are they don't dry out too much. warm, straigh

PALACE RICE

This recipe comes from Cambodia at a time when they had palaces. While using very similar ingredients to the Indonesian dish, this method produces a lighter result.

2 eggs
45 ml (3 tbs) cooking oil
1 bunch spring onions, trimmed and finely chopped
225 g (8 oz) cold cooked chicken (boned)
100 g (4 oz) prawns

225 g (8 oz) frozen peas
15 ml (1 tbs) soy sauce
225 g (8 oz) cold cooked rice
15 ml (1 tbs) sesame oil (see Ingredients, page 6)
30 ml (2 tbs) coriander or parsley, chopped

Beat the eggs and heat the oil (but not the sesame oil) in a wok or large frying pan. Put in the spring onions and the chicken, cut into pieces, and fry till hot. Add the prawns and peas and cook for 2 minutes. Pour in the eggs and allow to set before breaking up, so that the eggs absorb all the available liquid. Season with the soy sauce and add the rice, turning and stirring it until it's cooked right through and the chicken and prawns are distributed evenly through the rice. Serve immediately, sprinkling over the sesame oil, and garnishing with parsley or fresh coriander.

FALAFEL

Falafel are a kind of vegetarian meatball which are eaten all over the Middle East in various forms. They're traditionally eaten with pitta bread.

225 g (8 oz) chick peas (soaked for 6 hours
in 1 litre/2 pints water)
1 onion
1 clove garlic

oil for frying
5 ml (1 tsp) turmeric
2.5 ml (½ tsp) each chilli powder, paprika
and ground cumin

In a food processor or liquidizer, or in a mincer if you prefer, grind the chick peas with the onion, garlic, and enough oil to help the blades work. Stir into this mixture all the spices, and check the consistency: it should be firm enough to shape, with a spoon or wet hands, into balls or mini-hamburgers, about the size of a walnut. Deep fry these in hot oil for about 5 minutes until well browned, or shallow fry for 4–5 minutes a side. Serve with shredded lettuce and tomatoes, lemon juice to squeeze over, houmous or yoghurt to act as a sauce, and stuffed into warm pitta.

FILLED TACOS

Tacos are the Mexican answer to pitta. The traditional bread in Mexico is called a tortilla and, unlike the Spanish equivalent from which its name derives, it has no eggs in it, but is a flat pancake made of maize flour. It's a very versatile pancake though, since it can be made firm and crisp or soft and pliable. In the case of the taco version, the newly made pancake is folded over and, using a special pair of tongs, dipped into hot oil so that it's fried into a permanent folded shape, ideal for holding fillings. Tacos are quite difficult to make but are readily available from any supermarket. The filling is what makes the difference and here I do have a great idea. One word of warning: tacos are not tidy things to eat, so make sure that you have plenty of napkins on hand. They are great fun to eat though and are a good ice-breaker at parties.

700 g (1½ lb) minced beef *5 ml (1 tsp) garlic salt*
60 ml (4 tbs) tomato purée *2.5 ml (½ tsp) ground cumin*
15 ml (1 tbs) chilli sauce *12 taco shells*

Garnishing

1 iceberg lettuce *150 g (6 oz) grated Cheddar or Monterey*
2 tomatoes *Jack cheese*

Fry the meat in a non-stick pan until well browned. Add the tomato purée, chilli and seasonings and stir till well mixed. You may need a couple of tablespoons of water at this stage to make the mixture stick together. Warm the tacos briefly (5 minutes) in a medium oven, then spoon 2–3 tablespoons of the meat mixture into the base of each taco shell. Top with a layer of shredded lettuce, tomato slices and a tablespoon of the cheese.

RAITA

The classic yoghurt salad that accompanies every meal in north India, from a simple chapati to a lavish feast, owes its success to the combination of vegetables, and the refreshing tartness of the yoghurt.

2 ripe tomatoes
10 cm (4 in) piece cucumber, quartered lengthways and finely sliced
3 spring onions, trimmed and finely sliced

15 ml (1 tbs) lemon juice
125 ml (5 fl oz) plain yoghurt
5 ml (1 tsp) salt
15 ml (1 tbs) fresh coriander, chopped

Cut the tomatoes into pea-sized pieces in a bowl to save the juice, then add the onion and cucumber slices. Stir the lemon juice into the yoghurt with the salt and mix with the vegetables. Stir in the chopped coriander.

COCONUT CHUTNEY

In many southern Indian meals this forms an enormously popular condiment, eaten in spoonfuls with rice, pancakes or moist vegetable dishes.

150 g (6 oz) desiccated coconut
90 ml (6 tbs) hot water
15 ml (1 tbs) lemon juice
2 spring onions, trimmed and cut into 1 cm (1/2 in) slices

15 ml (1 tbs) brown sugar
15 ml (1 tbs) paprika
1.25 ml (1/4 tsp) each chilli powder and salt

Put the coconut in a bowl, add the hot water and lemon juice, and leave for 10 minutes. Put the coconut mixture into a food processor or liquidizer and process until a fine purée. Add all the other ingredients and process again for 10 seconds. Decant into a serving bowl and leave for 30 minutes at least, to absorb all the flavours.

SALSAS

The classic sauces or *salsa* of Mexican cookery make an appearance on every table, simple or grand. The origins, both of the red *salsas*, and of the green version below, lie in pre-Columbian Mexico and its great empires: Aztec, Olmec, Maya. They built great cities and developed sophisticated mathematics, but they also developed the most amazing range of crops. Peppers and tomatoes of all sorts are two of their crowning glories, so it's not surprising that the best loved sauces should be based on these vegetables. The green sauce needs Mexican green 'husk' tomatoes which are ripe when still green (our unripe ones won't do). Ask for them from speciality food shops that sell Mexican foods. They are canned on quite a large scale. These are not gentle dishes, so use them with discretion!

Red Salsa Cruda

100 g (4 oz) ripe tomatoes, chopped
75 g (3 oz) onions, peeled and chopped
2 small red or green chilli peppers: Serrano if possible
1 clove garlic, peeled
15 ml (1 tbs) oil

½ sweet red pepper, de-seeded and cut in four
2.5 ml (½ tsp) each salt and pepper
15 ml (1 tbs) chopped parsley or fresh coriander

Put all the ingredients into a food processor or liquidizer and process until a rough purée. Pour out and serve at room temperature.

Green Salsa Cruda

225 g (8 oz) Mexican green tomatoes, roughly chopped
4 spring onions, trimmed and chopped
2 small green chillies, Serrano if possible

½ green sweet pepper, de-seeded and roughly chopped
5 ml (1 tsp) salt
15 ml (1 tbs) fresh coriander, chopped

Put the tomatoes in a food processor or liquidizer and process till finely chopped. Add the other ingredients and process again for 10 seconds. Pour out and serve at room temperature; it will keep in the fridge for a week.

PICKLED VEGETABLES

These are eaten at the end of almost all Japanese meals with rice and green tea, as a kind of mouth refresher.

150 g (6 oz) cabbage
100 g (4 oz) carrots
half an onion
3 sticks celery
100 g (4 oz) turnip

½ cucumber
15 ml (1 tbs) salt
½ cup cider vinegar
½ cup water
30 ml (2 tbs) apple juice or Mirin

Peel the onion, carrot and turnip, trim the other vegetables and slice into 5 mm (¼ in) slices. Mix the pickling ingredients together, pour over the vegetables and put in a bowl into which a small plate will fit to press the mixture down. Put a 500 g (1 lb) weight or tin on the plate and leave for at least 6 hours and up to 3 days. Use a spoonful per person after a meal.

GUACAMOLE

This is the 'mole' or sauce of the *aguacate*, the old Mexican word for avocado. There are many variations, by means of adding more chilli, or green tomatoes, or no tomatoes.

1 ripe avocado, halved
2 spring onions, trimmed and coarsely chopped
½ each red and green pepper, de-seeded and cut into chunks

1 large ripe tomato, coarsely chopped
15 ml (1 tbs) each lime juice and olive oil
1.25 ml (¼ tsp) chilli pepper

Keep the avocado stone, and scoop out the flesh with a spoon. Put the onions, pepper and tomato into a liquidizer or food processor and process till roughly chopped. Add the other ingredients and season. Process for another 10 seconds. Add to a bowl with the stone and cover with clingfilm to help prevent browning. Eat with tortilla chips.

LIME CORDIAL

This is a home-made version of the kind of lime cordial that made Roses famous. In fact lime cordial was originally developed by Mr Rose as a means of preserving the juice for consumption off the islands. In its original form it was quite a complicated process but this method produces a delicious and refreshing drink which should be kept in the fridge if you are going to use it after more than two or three days.

12 limes
500 ml (1 pint) boiling water
1 cinnamon stick

350 g (12 oz) caster sugar
100 g (4 oz) brown sugar

Halve the limes and squeeze out the juice. Put the squeezed shells into a large china jug and pour the boiling water on top. Allow to marinate with the cinnamon stick for exactly 10 minutes. Strain into a saucepan and stir in both the sugars, and let it stand until the sugar has dissolved. Bring the mixture to the boil and, as soon as it is boiling, pour in the squeezed lime juice and take the pan off the heat. Store in a bottle or bottles that you have sterilised with baby bottle solution and then rinsed in boiling water. You can drink it as soon as it has cooled, but it matures after 2 or 3 days. Keep the lime cordial in the fridge and dilute it to taste with still, fizzy or hot water, or use as part of a punch.

Tea and Coffee

Tea and coffee are the most universally consumed drinks in the world after plain water. From Peking to Boston tea is drunk, from Finland to the tip of South Africa coffee prepared. The flavours differ as do the methods of preparation, and exotic variations are not lacking, whether it's the addition of Yak butter to tea in Tibet or egg shells to coffee in Sweden. But consume them we do in huge quantities, between meals, with meals, sometimes as the basis for meals.

Tea and coffee are huge business, they create vast industries, huge transport systems and some of the world's most important financial trading markets. Yet when all that is said and done, it comes down to what is in the cup in your hand. A hot (or usually hot) beverage that comforts, refreshes and sustains to the extent that nothing else in the world of food matches.

TEA

Tea com·· ·· ·· the le··ves of a species of Camellia bush. It grows in most climates but in commer··· ···ms only ·ropical or sub-tropical temperatures produce tea of a sufficiently good ···li··· ···· ···h···· ···· ··g on a large scale. It's also, for reasons that no-one seems to be able to ··· ··· ···· ays of b··tter quality if it's grown at high altitude. The tea grown above ···· ··· ···et is very much the most prized. So much of the tea we drink is grown in ···· ···· Ceylon and Ke··ya.

···· drunk it seems in China, around A.D. 300 or 400 and has continued to be drunk ··· ··nce with the largest production of tea in the world still occurring in China itself, ···le of it is exported these days. The western taste came when the Dutch and the British ···ies Companies, trading with China in the late 17th and 18th centuries, began to import it ··· ·d the rest of Western Europe. The European taste for tea was sudden and prodigious. ···, just 20,000 lbs was imported into Britain. A century later, by 1800, 20 million lbs a year ·· being consumed in the United Kingdom alone. So great was the demand that both the ··it·sh and the Dutch 'exported' tea production to their own colonies in the Far East – the British to Ir·lia and the Dutch to Indonesia – both of which remain to this day huge suppliers of tea, along ··· the other former British colonies of Ceylon and Kenya.

··a always was very big business. The Cutty Sark and the other great tea clippers which have ·· legend w··re designed to carry the first of the year's growths from China to Europe at the

Wilkinson's, Norwich, a specialist tea and coffee shop

COFFEE

⊠▩▨▨✦▨▩▨▩▨✦▨▩⊠

Coffee is perhaps the most unlikely drink that human beings consume. Consider for a m
likelihood of a tree producing a cherry-like fruit with two small green seeds. The seec
removed from the pulp of the fruit, then dried, then roasted, then ground very fine, a
water poured over them at boiling point, the subsequent liquid being filtered before
In fact, this very complex process didn't really develop it seems until about A.D.
Ethiopian area of Africa. There are all sorts of legends about how a goat-herd fir
coffee by noticing how frisky his goats were when they ate the cherry-like fruit and
himself, getting the caffeine bonus even from the raw seeds; the caffeine that has be
central part of the attraction and development of coffee.

In fact, the coffee seed seems to have been used in an unroasted or ground forn
food in the area for some centuries before, as it's rich both in carbohydrates and pro
the trick of roasting, grinding and brewing was discovered the drink itself spr
Constantinople from the Arabian peninsular and from there via Vienna to Wester
Arabs attempted to maintain a control over this very profitable trade route but, a
British, the Dutch and, on this occasion, the French discovered that they could gro cof
in their tropical colonies. Again, as with tea, a high altitude produces the best re .ts a
day, the Indonesian and Jamaican coffees that were the result of this pirating are son
in the world. At the beginning of the 18th century the bean was introduced to South
soon Brazil was to dominate the production of coffee. Today, more than half the
world comes from Brazil, which is a formidable consideration when you realise th   offee, afte
oil, is the second most valuable traded commodity in the whole world. Today, co   also growr
commercially in a number of other parts of South America, particularly Colc   ia, and also ir
Africa around Kenya and Tanzania.

Coffee drinking has long had a very mixed social reception. Coffee houses, w en they spread all
over Europe in the 17th Century, were often regarded with some suspicion, i deed Charles II of
England, who appeared to ban very little else, attempted to ban coffee hous s, and on the 23 d
December 1675 made that ban law. Such was the outcry in London at the tir e that by the 8th of
January 1676 he'd had to rescind it. Indeed, London coffee houses went on o create some of the
great institutions of the modern financial world – Lloyds of London, the insurance centre for
example, is named after the gentleman who established the coffee house in which the earliest
insurance brokers met to conduct their business.

Coffee is drunk in a wide variety of circumstances, both for the pleasure of its flavour and for its
digestive qualitites, and also for the boost to concentration, attention and, astonishingly enough,
muscular strength that the caffeine it contains gives. It's also drunk in a wide variety of ways, with
or without milk, with or without the grounds mixed in, and is perhaps made in the widest variety
of methods of any major drink.

Pots galore